More Praise for *Rising Together*

"I personally used key insights from *How Women Rise* to help foster diversity when I was CEO of Best Buy. Now Sally has done it again, providing an indispensable guide for changing behaviors in a way that helps everyone rise. A must read for every leader."

—Hubert Joly, former Best Buy CEO, author of *The Heart of Business*, senior lecturer at Harvard Business School

"*Rising Together* is the perfect guide to building equitable, safe, and diverse workspaces today. In her signature conversational voice, Sally helps us gain greater awareness of the triggers and the habits that hold us back so we can build relationships that can help us all rise. A must-read for veterans and newcomers in business!"

—Sanyin Siang, CEO Coach, Thinkers50 Top Management Thinker, and author of *The Launch Book*

"If you want to be an inclusive leader, *Rising Together* is your GPS. Sally Helgesen will help you elevate your inclusion game, foster team trust at a faster rate, and build a new generation of leaders."

—Erica Dhawan, *Wall Street Journal* bestselling author of *Digital Body Language*

"Sally Helgesen has spent 35 years working with women around the world to advance their careers. With *Rising Together,* she draws on this rich experience to show how all of us can most effectively support colleagues across a range of boundaries."

—Minda Harts, author of *The Memo* and *You Are More Than Magic*

"As women become vitally important throughout the workforce, it's time to look at the mindset, behaviors, and habits that create inclusivity. Sally's book, based on her decades of research, helps us pinpoint opportunities for individuals and organizations to truly 'Rise Together.'"

—Josh Bersin, Global HR Industry Analyst

RISING TOGETHER

HOW WE CAN **BRIDGE DIVIDES**
AND CREATE A
MORE INCLUSIVE WORKPLACE

RISING
Together

SALLY HELGESEN

Go
hachette
BOOKS

New York

Hachette Go, an imprint of Hachette Books
Hachette Book Group
1290 Avenue of the Americas
New York, NY 10104
HachetteGo.com
Facebook.com/HachetteGo
Instagram.com/HachetteGo

First Edition: February 2023

Hachette Books is a division of Hachette Book Group, Inc.

The Hachette Go and Hachette Books name and logos are trademarks of Hachette Book Group, Inc.

The publisher is not responsible for websites (or their content) that are not owned by the publisher.

Print book interior design by Amy Quinn.

Library of Congress Control Number: 2022920630

ISBNs: 978-0-306-82830-0 (hardcover); 978-0-306-82832-4 (ebook)

Printed in the United States of America

LSC-C

Printing 1, 2022

For Marshall Goldsmith
Friend, colleague, all-around source of inspiration and support
No one is better at the art and practice of Rising Together

Contents

Part II: A Culture of Belonging

Acknowledgments

My deepest thanks go to my agent Jim Levine, who encouraged—indeed, hounded—me to write this book for ten years. And to Courtney Paganelli, who works with Jim and came up with the perfect title, while encouraging me to update my frame of reference.

I am also grateful to Edward Tivnan, who gave me timely and professional book doctor support when I needed it most.

Thanks to my superb editor Lauren Marino, who went the extra mile and broadened my sense of this book's subject, and to publisher Mary Ann Naples, who saw the potential and offered support. I know from experience how strong the team at Hachette is, and look forward to working with you all as we move forward.

Huge thanks to my own team: Luke Joerger, Isaac Bush, and the people at Hastings Digital Media, as well as my sister Cece Helgesen, whose marketing insights set things humming. Thanks to my assistant Cynthia Gray, who wrangles logistics and so I have time to write, and to Robert Trevellyan, on whose tech skills I rely every day.

Thanks to all my colleagues in the 100 Coaches network, especially those whom I interviewed for this book: John Baldoni, Chris Cappy, Bill Carrier, Patricia Gorton, Ruth Gotian, Jeffrey Hull, Terry Jackson, Tom Kolditz, Lindsey Pollak, Diane Ryan, Molly Tschang, Eddie Turner, and Bev Wright. And to Scott Osman, who makes the network a dependable joy.

Special thanks to Nancy Badore, Tom Peters, Art Kleiner, and of course Marshall Goldsmith for their career-spanning support. And to the many clients whose stories inform this book.

I am so grateful to my husband, Bart Gulley; my peer coach and friend-for-life Elizabeth Bailey; and to Marilyn Bethany and the whole Tivnan/Bethany clan, who served as my family during the pandemic. And to my always-in-touch Helgesen siblings.

Finally, I am indebted to dear late friends and colleagues Stanley Crouch and Roosevelt Thomas, whose thinking becomes more prescient with each passing day.

A Note on Names

The stories in this book are drawn from my many decades of working with clients around the world. In these stories, I use only first names and have changed some details to protect privacy.

I also sought insights from dozens of leadership coaches, authors, and experts, drawn from my rich global network. These individuals are identified by their full names.

Foreword

by Marshall Goldsmith

Sally Helgesen's amazing career has resulted in her becoming the world's premier authority on women's leadership and the #1 ranked coach for women leaders. Along with her classic works, *The Female Advantage* and *The Web of Inclusion*, she has most recently been the lead author of *How Women Rise*, one of the most widely read and critically acclaimed books for women in the workplace ever written.

With *Rising Together*, Sally takes her contribution to the next level, going beyond what women can do to succeed to focus on what we all can do to help one another build more satisfying careers and create a better world. Leaders everywhere who seek to move their teams, organizations, and relationships beyond infighting and blame and achieve positive partnerships can benefit from the wisdom in this book. Given today's divisive environment, the timing could not be better.

Both Sally and I were mentored by the great Peter Drucker, the founder of modern management. Peter taught us, "We spend a lot of time teaching leaders what to do. We do not spend enough time teaching leaders what to stop." In *Rising Together*, Sally does an incredibly thorough job of teaching leaders both what to stop and what to do by taking actions that create fruitful results.

In my *New York Times* bestseller *Triggers*, I show how our environment can set off positive or negative reactions that dramatically impact our behavior and how others perceive us. Sally goes well beyond my work to describe the most common triggers that inhibit our ability to form strong relationships across bounds. One of my favorite chapters, "It's Not Fair," graphically illustrates how our expectations can stir resentments that keep us, and everyone around us, stuck.

Sally also moves beyond buzzwords and exhortation to provide highly specific and original practices for creating what she calls cultures of belonging. Her emphasis on behavior as opposed to bias—on what we do as opposed to what we think—has been missing from most diversity conversations and has the potential to transform them.

I've had the honor of knowing and working with Sally for over twenty-five years. She has never stopped growing as a professional and as a person. In *Rising Together*, she brings together decades of research, teaching, and coaching from every corner of the globe in order to build upon and extend her previous work.

To me, brilliance is the ability to create something that seems obvious and should have been done years ago—but has never been done. *Rising Together* meets this definition of brilliance. In hindsight, we should have had this book decades ago. It's long overdue, but it's just what our world needs now.

Thank you, Sally!

Introduction

The How of Solidarity

A few years ago, I was scheduled to deliver a women's leadership program at the Construction SuperConference in Las Vegas, a premier annual event for the industry. Given that I've delivered hundreds of such programs at conferences around the world, I had a preconceived notion of what I would encounter. I expected a hundred or so women who worked in a heavily male industry where they struggled to feel noticed, appreciated, and valued. I anticipated that they'd be eager for insights on how to build their careers and forge needed support in the face of skepticism or indifference.

My expectations were confounded when I arrived at the hotel conference room to discover a huge, standing-room-only crowd that was around 60 percent male. I'd been told, as I had on many similar occasions, to expect men in the audience. But typically only a handful showed up.

Given the high male turnout in Las Vegas, my prepared program felt misjudged, so I asked the male participants what had inspired them to attend this session. A forest of hands shot up. "A lot of the best talent these days is female," a burly project manager explained. "But we have a hard time hiring women. And the ones we do hire often leave. If we can't figure out how to become better places for women to work, we're not going to have much of a future."

One executive was particularly blunt. "We hope you're not going to waste your time making the case for *why* developing and retaining women is important for our industry," he said. "We know all about the whys. What we don't know is *how* to do it. We haven't got a clue."

Rising Together is my response to that executive's plea to provide some hows.

And the hows matter. Because when it comes to building honest and fruitful relationships across potential divides—not only of gender but of race, ethnicity, sexuality, and by generation—everyone is seeking clues.

Given the increasing diversity of the workplace in every corner of the globe, we all need to develop the skills required to build strong relationships with people we may view as different from ourselves. This is true whether we're senior leaders, managers, individual contributors, new hires, entrepreneurs, professional service providers, supervisors, or gig workers.

The ability to adeptly build such relationships gives us a way to demonstrate appreciation and goodwill in situations that might otherwise be awkward, volatile, or confusing. It keeps us engaged and in the flow even as the world shifts around us. And it helps us create the kind of harmonious all-hands-on-deck teams that high-performing organizations rely upon.

This is to everyone's advantage.

My purpose in writing *Rising Together* is to address the challenge of building broad, resilient, and diverse webs of relationship in two ways.

The first part of the book identifies eight common triggers that undermine our ability to connect with people whose history and values may be different from our own. These triggers get activated when situations, expectations, misapprehensions, or fears prevent us from responding in ways we intuitively know would serve us and those around us. Instead we retreat to our comfort zone, which keeps us stuck.

But identifying potential barriers is only the first step. We also need to take positive action. That's why the second part of this book offers simple and very specific everyday practices that enable us—as individuals, in our organizations, on our teams—to create cultures of belonging.

This term, culture of belonging, may sound fuzzy or idealistic. And yet it can be clearly defined.

A culture of belonging is one in which the largest possible percentage of people:

- Feel ownership in the organization, viewing it as "we," not "they"
- Believe they are valued for their *potential* as well as their contributions
- Perceive that how they matter is not strictly tied to their positional power

The key question is: *How* can these feelings, beliefs, and perceptions be instilled?

In my experience, behaviors and actions are the key. This contrasts with the emphasis on mind-sets, assumptions, and the search for unconscious biases that has become the dominant means for addressing diversity in organizations in recent years.

Viewing inclusion as a practice, a how, enshrined in specific behaviors, makes it concrete and achievable rather than a vague aspiration or a well-intentioned expression of generalized goodwill. It also makes it measurable:

- If you hear someone talking about his company or its leaders as "they," you can bet he's not experiencing it as inclusive.
- If someone says her boss has little idea of her real talents, you can take it to the bank she doesn't feel a part of a supportive team.

- If your team members say they believe only muckety-mucks get a hearing, you may be earning a D on the inclusion front.

THE FIERCE URGENCY OF THIS PARTICULAR MOMENT

The need to create cultures of belonging is urgent now, given the unprecedented willingness of people to walk away from workplaces in which they feel undervalued, disconnected, or burnt out. Yet the pressure on retention, which is rooted in widespread disengagement, is hardly new. Gallup's annual State of the Global Workplace poll found that only 15 percent of employees reported feeling actively engaged by their work in 2019. So it's hardly surprising that the added pressures of the pandemic would set off the exodus of workers that's become known as The Great Resignation or The Great Attrition.

This was a crisis waiting to happen. And it's created a fresh imperative for organizations, and for every one of us, to get better at inclusion and belonging. This is the challenge of our historical moment.

The practice-based approach I advocate in this book derives from my direct experience. I have spent the last thirty-five years working in thirty-eight countries around the globe, always with a dual mission. I help women and other traditional outsiders to recognize, articulate, and act on their greatest strengths and identify the internal barriers that could hold them back. And I help organizations build inclusive cultures that enable the largest possible number of people to contribute their best talents.

This work has given me the opportunity to interview thousands of people in wildly varied settings.

I've spent the afternoon in a courtyard on Zamalek island in Cairo where women arrayed from head to toe in sky blue shucked corn as they discussed their professional aspirations.

I've sat up into the wee hours in Tokyo sushi bars where senior executives loosened their ties, ordered another round of sake, and bemoaned the cultural constraints that keep their organizations stuck.

I've listened to female artificial intelligence engineers in Silicon Valley and Singapore—among the most educated and skilled women on the planet—describe their fear of being perceived as "too ambitious" if they speak directly about their skills and aspirations.

And I've been approached by African American men eager to compare their experiences with traditional white male leaders to those faced by the women Marshall Goldsmith and I describe in our book *How Women Rise.*

These and thousands of other disparate encounters have convinced me that there's never been a better time for us to collaborate broadly on helping one another to rise. Given the whiplash instability and economic tensions that have been a hallmark of the 2020s so far, this may strike some as wildly optimistic, especially given the very real divisions that the disruptions that the last fifteen years have kicked up.

Yet as I saw in Las Vegas, and as I hear on my travels, organizations have grown increasingly serious about doing what it takes to engage the broadest possible range of people. Leaders no longer expect, as many did even twenty years ago, that a highly diverse workforce will simply adjust to business as usual, or that people will repress what is distinctive about themselves in an effort to fit in. As the chief information officer (CIO) of a *Fortune* 100 manufacturing company based in the Midwest recently confided, "We've finally gotten the message that we need to meet our people where they are. And that *we* have a lot to learn from *them*."

Just as important, individuals in companies who once may have felt like outsiders, unsure of their role or their prospects, have become far more assured of the value they have to contribute and more determined to be recognized for their potential. Growing confidence at all levels is in fact one of the primary reasons that people are increasingly willing to abandon jobs that may look good on paper but which they perceive as demeaning, unsatisfying, a poor fit for their talents, or a potential dead end.

This strengthened confidence has also led to greater solidarity as those who in the past were perceived as outsiders have become more eager to support one another and more skilled at doing so.

Solidarity is an old-fashioned word, long associated with labor or student strikes, that needs to be retrofitted for an era when the forces of division are active but the benefits of coming together are obvious and strong. Solidarity arises when we focus on what we have in common and what we are trying to achieve—our shared roots and shared purpose—rather than highlighting what divides us or where we may feel shortchanged. Although solidarity is often born out of painful experience, it always looks *forward* to what can be done.

Social movements such as Black Lives Matter and MeToo have been key to strengthening solidarity in our era, giving public expression to bitter forms of exclusion that were rarely shared and routinely glossed over. So too have the networks, initiatives, and employee resource groups that have evolved in organizations around the globe. They have given a voice and a forum to those who were formerly expected to simply adapt.

In the past, many who held senior positions were reluctant to join or even publicly support these initiatives. For example, during the 1990s, I was often asked by client companies to try to drum up support from high-level women for network events that served female employees at less senior levels. The majority who declined noted that they had "worked hard to be seen as a leader, not a woman," and feared that signing on would undermine their hard-won status.

Today, senior female leaders are more likely to view supporting women at less senior levels as an opportunity to distinguish themselves, enhance their visibility, and build useful connections. In sum, a good career move. And because many senior women have by now benefited from these initiatives, they regard participation as a way to "pay it forward" by actively advocating for those who are coming up.

I see a similar evolution in networks that serve people of color and sexual minorities.

History teaches that solidarity is powerful, with amplifying effects that can transform even situations that seem hopelessly entangled. Whereas mighty organizations—or nations, for that matter—can be quickly paralyzed by infighting and division, extraordinary things can happen at warp speed when people come together and focus on the *we* instead of the *they*.

BACK TO THE HOW

As noted, *Rising Together* identifies both the triggers that can undermine this evolution as well as the practices that support it. I believe this practice-based approach is powerful precisely because it is rooted in everyday experience rather than policy or theory. It offers a bottom-up path to change that gives every one of us the opportunity to shape the cultures of which we are a part.

It's also more helpful than the mind-set or unconscious bias approach because it relies upon the observable truth that people are more immediately affected by how we behave toward them—our actions—than by whatever happens to be running through our minds at the moment. In addition, it's usually easier to try out new behaviors than to attempt to shift our internal thoughts. Practicing new behaviors increases the likelihood that we will elicit different responses from those around us, which in turn can result in our having different experiences. These experiences may then start to shift our thinking in a more organic way.

We're all familiar with how this works.

For example, we think we don't like a particular person. In response, an unconscious bias may kick in. As a result, we find ourselves meditating not only on why we don't like *this* person, but why we don't particularly care for this *kind* of person.

Then we have an encounter with this person in which we try, however awkwardly, to act in a more open and affirming way. We get a positive response, and soon discover that we have a number of things in common. We begin to revise our previous opinion of this particular person. And over time, we may begin to rethink the assumptions we've been making about others whom we've assumed to be in some way *like them*.

This mental evolution reflects a simple truth: that it's easier to act our way into a new way of thinking than to think our way into a new way of acting.

This is why *Rising Together* asks us to consider how making small behavioral tweaks might support our ability to expand the workplace relationships that shape our careers and enrich our daily lives. Such an expansion can broaden our influence while also making us bigger people—more capacious, more open, more at ease in the world.

PART I

Eight Common Triggers

CHAPTER ONE

The Nature of Triggers

*We rise together by understanding the common
triggers that can hold us back*

For decades, I've watched specific situations trigger negative perceptions and reactions between men and women at work. These situations are so routine they've come to feel like scenes from a play I've sat through too many times.

SCENE ONE

A woman—let's call her Jen—shares an idea during a meeting of her extended team. Nobody acknowledges her or says a word in response. Ten minutes later, a male colleague—let's call him Mark—makes the same point and is quickly recognized: "Great idea, Mark! Can you tell us how that would work?"

Jen is irritated that Mark is being credited with an idea she has put forth, but reluctant to stir the pot by pointing it out. After all, isn't the *idea* what really matters, not who gets the credit? And if she says something, won't she just seem petty? She doesn't want to sound aggrieved or, God forbid, come off as a victim. And there's no sense in making an enemy of Mark. So she tries to ignore her resentment and tells herself to move on.

Yet as the meeting progresses, Jen finds herself recalling other times when something similar has happened, to her or to other women in the company. These recollections feed her resentment and compound her sense of being invisible and undervalued. By the time the meeting's over, she's stewing.

In the hall outside, she grabs her friend Chantal and lets loose. "Can you *believe* how everyone responded as if my suggestion was Mark's idea? I've seen the same thing happen to you. The guys here are incapable of hearing anything a woman says!"

SCENE TWO

Jason tells his junior colleague Kim that he'd like to recommend her for a position posted on their company's internal network. He thinks she'd be perfect for the job. He also likes building the kind of give-and-take relationships that boost others while increasing the power of his network and establishing connections that may prove useful for him in the future. In addition, the company has been encouraging men to more actively engage women as allies, so this seems like an opportunity to score some points.

But Kim hesitates, saying she needs time to think about it. Jason wonders what there is to think about, but agrees. Then a few days later, Kim stops by his office to tell him that, while she appreciates his offer, she doesn't feel ready for the new position. "I took a look at the posting and I don't have all the skills they list," she says. "Plus I've still got things to learn about the job I'm in now."

Jason has heard Kim underplay her abilities in the past and views her line about needing to master all the skills before she even applies for a new job as a lame excuse. He wonders whether she's one of those women who lack ambition. Just last month, another female colleague turned down a promotion that would have positioned her for a director-level position. What's up with that? The company's trying to push women forward but women seem to be pushing back.

He's disappointed and decides to write Kim off.

These are stock scenarios. Versions of them happen all the time. What they have in common is that they usually trigger stock responses. Stock responses are rooted in the observations and experiences that shape our expectations without our even being aware of it. We interpret what is happening now through the lens of what we've observed (or think we've observed) in the past, or our beliefs about how other people—or the world—*should* be.

This is normal. It's how we as humans operate. Stock responses appeal to us because they offer handy mental shortcuts for dealing with circumstances that routinely crop up. They feel easy because they're familiar and they feel satisfying because they confirm what we're already primed to believe. But because they deprive us of intention and choice, stock responses undermine our ability to address routine situations that can trigger us at any moment.

My colleague Marshall Goldsmith literally wrote the book on triggers: incidents that provoke us, stir emotion, and cause us to respond in ways that may further inflame our situation and that rarely serve our interests. Marshall identifies a trigger as any stimulus or situation that shapes our thoughts, words, or actions. He notes that triggers are environmental. That is, they lie outside ourselves.

Because of this, we can't control the events that trigger us. But we can control how we respond. If we don't, we essentially cede power to our environment and allow ourselves to be dominated by random words and actions. We permit ourselves to be ambushed by circumstance. We inhibit our own ability to change and grow.

Triggers operate in a wide range of situations. We can be triggered while driving ("Did you see what that idiot just did?") or by a family member ("I can't believe you're bringing this up again!"). In this book, we are primarily concerned with how common triggers can diminish our ability to build constructive relationships across a wide range of divides. And since both our workplaces and our communities are growing ever more diverse, learning to identify and defuse such triggers will become an increasingly indispensable skill.

Failing to address the kind of common triggers that the workplace throws at us can deprive us of helpful allies, limit our capacity for collaboration, diminish our job performance, and stunt our careers. It can also undermine the health of our teams and cause dysfunction in our organizations. The impact of triggers can be individual (we fail to reach our full potential) or systemic (our company gets embroiled in a messy lawsuit). But whatever the scope of the damage, giving triggers free rein holds us back from being the people we'd like to be, and from building workplaces in which everyone can thrive.

The emphasis in universities in recent years on encouraging people to shield themselves and others from potential triggers does a huge disservice to students who will soon find themselves in a workplace where the ability to deal with a range of people is expected and required. Instead of shying away from triggering situations, avoiding potentially sensitive encounters, or lobbing accusations, every one of us needs to build our awareness of their impact so we can find serviceable ways to respond. Treating ourselves as sensitive plants unable to handle situations that disturb us will seriously impair our ability to build fruitful relationships with those we perceive as different from ourselves. This will undermine our ability to create the kind of satisfying careers that give full scope to our talents.

THE STORIES WE TELL

In my experience, triggers are the prime reason that men and women end up retreating to gender silos, narrowing their experience and depriving themselves of useful connections. That's what happened when Jen enlisted Chantal to commiserate with her after the meeting in which Mark received credit for her idea. Sharing her resentment with a female colleague may have temporarily relieved the emotional distress Jen felt at being disregarded. But venting her feelings only reinforced the story she was telling herself to explain what had happened: *"Men just can't listen to women!"* This increased the likelihood of her remaining stuck in a negative groove.

It's the *stories* we tell ourselves when we feel triggered that keep us dug in and limit our ability to frame an effective response.

Here's how the process works:

First, the trigger kicks off an emotional reaction that blindsides us. We feel a rush of adrenaline, a sinking in the pit of our stomach, a recoil, a blinding rage, or a snide "of course." Or we may simply feel confusion. Our immediate impulse may be to lash out. But if we're in a work situation, we fear what this could cost us, so we try to suppress our feelings and move on. When this doesn't succeed, we may grab the first opportunity to complain to a sympathetic colleague, which is why so much time at work gets consumed in gripe sessions and unproductive gossip.

In this way, our response to triggers plays a role in shaping toxic cultures that set us against one another, justify sniping, and waste everybody's time.

But whether we suffer in silence or indulge the urge to vent, the one thing we almost always do when triggered is try to put what happened in some kind of context. This is where storytelling enters the picture. We craft a narrative based on past experience or perceptions in a way that assigns blame, exonerates us, and magnifies impact.

Because these stories make us feel better, we may not stop to question whether they are either accurate or useful. Yet the truth is that our go-to stories rarely serve us well. They are especially damaging when they operate across divides: gender, of course (*"Men can't, women just refuse"*), but also race, ethnicity, sexual orientation, and age (*"They always, they seem incapable of . . . "*).

Because these default stories rely on generalizations and stereotypes, they reinforce any biases we may have. This makes it difficult for us to see others in their particularity; instead, they appear to us as members of a group. In addition, because our go-to stories usually emphasize our own innocence (*"I had no idea!" "I never guessed he would . . . "*), they often reinforce our feelings of being aggrieved or victimized—an increasing hazard for men as well as women.

Since we can't control other people, our best path is to acknowledge the emotional and mental impact a trigger has on us. This necessary first step can then enable us to choose a response that enhances our dignity and serves our interests.

ALTERNATIVE SCRIPTS

Although triggering situations lie outside our control, the *stories* we tell ourselves about them do not. This is why devising a different story to explain what happened is the simplest and most effective means for creating the conditions that let us determine an effective response.

But first, we need to notice and accept that we're being triggered without framing it in a self-interested way.

- We don't tell ourselves *this shouldn't happen*. We accept that it did.
- We don't tell ourselves *I can't deal with this*. We accept that we need to.
- We don't tell ourselves *I can't believe this person would . . .* We accept that he did.

Practicing this kind of acceptance—otherwise known as getting real—gives us the measure of detachment required to create an alternative script that puts what just happened in a less volatile perspective.

Doing so is not Pollyanna-ish. Nor is it a form of denial. It's making a strategic decision based on the pragmatic recognition that a positive story puts *us* in control. After all, we are the ones choosing how to tell it. And we are the ones who get to decide what interpretation will best enable us to move forward.

Writing a positive script also arrests the train of automatic assumptions that our usual go-to stories reinforce. These familiar narratives confirm our right to feel undervalued, disrespected, or aggrieved. A fresh narrative, by contrast, gives us a way to push back against our own stuckness.

Let's look at how this process might have shifted the outcome in the two scenarios described earlier.

SCENE ONE

First of all, Jen would admit to herself that she was irritated by Mark's intervention rather than trying to repress what she was feeling or telling herself she should ignore it and move on. Instead, she would simply notice that Mark repeating her idea—and being acknowledged for it—had triggered a train of familiar thoughts and assumptions that seemed to explain what had happened:

- *Guys here have trouble hearing anything a woman says.*
- *Guys always stick together.*
- *There's no way I can push back without seeming petty.*
- *I feel disrespected and unheard but I am stuck.*

By contrast, recognizing that she was defaulting to an all-too-familiar internal dialogue would have enabled Jen to tell herself a story that supported her ability to feel respected and heard. By acknowledging without judgment that she felt undermined by what occurred, she could use a new story to give herself a path forward.

For example, she could tell herself that Mark may have reiterated her idea because he agreed with it and was trying to support her. Or she could decide that he was summarizing what she'd said in an effort to amplify it. These explanations, these stories, would enable her to give him the benefit of the doubt, the benefit of her goodwill, increasing the likelihood of a positive outcome.

Here's the thing: *It doesn't matter whether Jen believes this alternative story is true or not.* Even if she's pretty sure that Mark was trying to grab credit for her idea, creating a positive narrative helps her take power over the situation. Revising her script enables her to reinterpret a painful situation and gives her a number of ways to claim what she wants—in this case, recognition—without going to the mattresses by calling Mark out.

For example, as soon as Mark spoke, Jen could respond: "I'm so glad Mark agrees with what I just said. Thank you, Mark!" Then, instead of grabbing Chantal for an ultimately unproductive gripe session, she could intercept Mark as the meeting broke up: "It's great to know you and I think alike on this issue. I'd love to discuss how we could move ahead."

Even if Jen felt too blindsided to respond constructively in the moment, she could still make the situation work to her advantage by taking action after the fact. For example, she could email Mark the next morning to say how pleased she was that he agreed with her idea and suggest they set a time to explore joining forces.

Please note that taking these positive actions gives Jen the chance to claim the idea she put forth as her own. Not exclusively hers, of course—Mark is now in the picture. But reworking her story lets her put a stake in the ground rather than just taking the loss or fuming with resentment, approaches that increase the likelihood of her getting left on the sidelines. Plus she puts Mark and everyone else who witnessed the exchange on notice that she is not about to let herself be discounted or run over.

In my experience, this kind of approach often inspires the other person to actually start believing the new story line themselves. Why wouldn't they, when it supports their desire to have a positive self-image? Instead of being cast as your antagonist, they suddenly find themselves being viewed as your ally: "Hey, yeah, that's what I meant, I *was* trying to support you." Best of all, you engineered this sudden realization on their part. Talk about strategically asserting control!

The point is that, however forced or inauthentic this kind of interchange might feel in the moment, it's valuable because it serves your interests while also making the world a nicer place. It enables you to build a connection that might otherwise have eluded you. And it turns a potentially negative situation to your advantage.

How bad is that?

SCENE TWO

Jason felt blown off when Kim declined his offer to recommend her for the position he'd seen posted. She'd been a stellar contributor and he assumed she'd be eager to move up. Her reluctance baffled him but, given that another woman on his team had recently declined a promotion, he decided it must be part of a pattern. Women seemed happy to slog away doing huge amounts of work but less eager to go for the big wins or position themselves as players, which meant they didn't have much potential as allies. So even though the company was encouraging men to support them, Jason decided there really wasn't much point.

The situation might have developed differently if Jason had considered an alternative story.

- He could have told himself that, since Kim was one of only three female engineers in a division of seventy high-achieving men, she might not be accustomed to support and was unsure how to respond to his offer.

- He could have considered that Kim's habit of discounting her considerable abilities might stem from not having received positive feedback in the past, and resolved to make sure she got some in the future.

- He could have questioned whether her apparent belief that she had to have all the skills to qualify for a new position might be a misread of what was expected of someone applying for a new job rather than a lame excuse.

Working from any of these scripts would have given Jason a positive path forward. Instead of writing Kim off, he could have tried to get a better picture of how she experienced her work and what she wanted from her career. As coach and consultant Chris Cappy notes, "If you don't bother to ask the big questions—*what's important to you? What do you want from your work?*—you'll never know how you can help someone else. That means you sometimes have to push the conversation. It's what being an ally is all about."

If Jason hadn't jumped to the conclusion that Kim lacked ambition, he might have elicited ideas about how his team could work more effectively together as well as building a more productive relationship with Kim. This would have served her, but it would have served him as well. After all, the company *was* making a huge push on diversity, which meant that more women would be joining his team and more women would be assuming positions of power. Honing his skills as a supporter of women was likely to be a smart career move.

THE AUTHENTICITY TRAP

Devising a positive story to explain a triggering event is a simple but effective tool. It requires only that we put aside our defensive go-to assumptions (*"Mark's trying to steal my idea"*; *"Kim's never going to be a player"*) so we can put our energies into a constructive approach.

Positive scripts demand a certain generosity of spirit. We're giving someone the benefit of the doubt *even though we're not sure they've earned it*. This can feel like a stretch, but doing so expands our ability to build a broad range of relationships as well as the resilience required to keep going in times of stress.

Yet when I work with clients, I routinely get pushback on the alternative script approach. The most common objection? People perceive it as acting fake.

Typical comments include:

- "Why should I tell myself a made-up story about someone who's acting like a jerk? It seems dishonest and inauthentic."
- "I prefer being real to being phony. It's important to be true to myself."
- From men: "I'm not the politically correct type who caters to women. I call 'em as I see 'em."
- From women: "Why do *women* always have to adjust to male standards and male behavior? I have a right to act on what I believe!"

It's hardly surprising that, after a decade or more in which we have all been regularly exhorted to "bring our authentic selves" to work, we may view such tactics as a threat to our integrity. But being overly invested in our first responses increases our susceptibility to being triggered and limits our ability to frame an effective response.

I call this the authenticity trap.

Because we're committed to a specific vision of who we are—or who we believe we should be—we imagine that giving others the benefit of the doubt would constitute disloyalty to ourselves and betray our values. Whereas in fact, we would simply be trying out a new idea to see how it might work.

My colleague Marshall Goldsmith calls the authenticity trap "the excessive need to be me." He notes that an immoderate loyalty to our own self-definition stunts our ability to evolve, grow, and learn from our experiences. He views this kind of stubbornness (*That's just how I am!*") as a pointless vanity that holds us back from making changes that would help us and everyone around us.

Obviously, none of us benefits from pretending to be something or someone we're not. But writing an alternative script doesn't require this. It simply asks that we avoid buying into our first reaction to a situation so we can consider a range of explanations.

This is not being fake or phony or somehow untrue to ourselves. It is merely accepting that we may not have all the answers, that our immediate judgments may not be correct. And recognizing that, even if they are, *acting* on these judgments may not be our most effective path forward.

BEYOND BLINDSIDED

Another common objection to writing a positive script is the fear that doing so will make us vulnerable to manipulation. I hear this a lot. "If I give the benefit of the doubt to someone who is actually trying to undermine me, won't I be giving that person power at my own expense?"

We certainly would if we uncritically bought into our upbeat script. But this is not what we are doing. We are simply substituting a positive story for a negative one while remaining aware that both may have elements of truth. What's important to remember is that our new script is an interpretation that *we* are choosing to consider. This gives us the flexibility to switch gears if the situation requires.

It's also helpful to bear in mind that, even if someone is trying to undermine us, giving them the benefit of the doubt can still be highly effective. For one thing, it helps calm the adrenaline that floods our system whenever we feel under threat. This familiar fight-or-flight response is part of our human heritage, meant to protect us from predators and keep us alive. But it kicks in whenever we feel triggered, making it tough to respond in a way that serves us. Adrenaline—otherwise known as the heat of the moment—causes our pulse to race and our breathing to grow shallow. This clouds our thinking and puts us in a reactive state.

By contrast, assuming positive intent calms our reflexes, buying us time to ground ourselves and identify an intentional way to proceed. Instead of feeling blindsided, enraged, or helpless (*"How dare that jerk!"*), we have the bandwidth to consider a range of responses. Also, as noted earlier, people may change their behavior when we act as if we have no clue that they were actually intending to be antagonistic. They may find they prefer our version of what happened because it flatters their self-image and affirms them as a wonderful person.

Having been offered the benefit of the doubt, they may decide that acting as if they believe our positive story is the better course.

TRYING IT OUT

Teresa was the executive director of a regional museum association whom I was brought in to coach. She'd had a strong relationship with the previous board chair, but he'd resigned to deal with family issues shortly after she took the job. The new chair, Larry, immediately began to assert control by giving her a hard time at the board's monthly meetings.

Teresa would spend days preparing her presentation to the board, only to get pummeled by Larry for what he thought she'd gotten wrong. When she tried to explain her reasoning, he'd just double down. She thought his tactics made some of the other board members uncomfortable, but no one spoke up on her behalf, which made her feel isolated and disrespected. When he got going, she felt like fleeing the room.

I asked her what she thought was going on.

"He's a control freak," she declared. "Plus I happen to know he wanted someone else for my job. So now he's trying to prove I'm in over my head. And to tell the truth, I'm starting to feel that way myself. Basically, I think he wants to derail me in hopes that I'll just give up and go away."

I noted that her interpretation might be true. But this left the question of how she should handle the situation. Did she have any ideas?

"Maybe I should talk to a couple other board members, privately one-on-one. They might be able to get him to lay off."

I asked whether she thought doing so might be construed as her trying to divide the board or asking them to choose sides.

She agreed this was a possibility.

I asked whether she thought that any of the board members had real influence over Larry.

"Not really. He's the head of the biggest museum in the whole association and he's got the best connections with major donors and in the media. So everyone just gives him a pass."

Knowing this, and given the passivity the other board members had demonstrated in meetings, did she really expect one of them to confront him about his behavior?

"Probably not. Plus I could see it blowing up on me. But I can't think of anything else to do."

I suggested that Teresa consider reinterpreting Larry's behavior. What if she told herself that he was actually trying to make her a stronger leader by testing her publicly so she could toughen up? Even if this were not the case, it would give her the opportunity to treat him like a supporter whose comments she sought and valued. This might inspire him to change his approach.

"But wouldn't that make me seem craven and weak?" Teresa objected. "I could see losing credibility with the entire board."

I suggested that she might instead come across as unintimidated by Larry, curious about what she could learn from him. This might be a relief for everyone involved.

Teresa agreed to try the alternative script approach, acting as if she viewed Larry's needling as a helpful intervention. Because she was concerned about making herself vulnerable to a man she actually viewed as "kind of a killer," we decided we would work on her body language to prepare her for the next meeting.

The idea was that if Teresa could focus her efforts on standing her ground while Larry was speaking—inhabiting her space, meeting his eyes, and appearing to listen in a detached but thoughtful way—she would send a physical message (to herself, to Larry, and to everyone present) that she was open yet resilient, glad to learn but not intimidated by Larry's comments.

Teresa tried this at the next meeting. Afterward she reported, "I just focused on breathing deeply and slowly and kind of let his words roll over me while telling myself he was only trying to be helpful. This distracted me from panicking when he started in. It's like my mind got the message from my body that I could handle his aggression. This made me feel stronger, which was the opposite of what I'd expected."

As Teresa continued this practice over the next few months, she found that she felt calm enough to identify when Larry was actually making some helpful points. "I began asking him for clarification when he said something I thought I could learn from and told myself to ignore the rest. I didn't feel craven doing this because I was in control of myself. *I* was the one who was writing the script for how I participated in our meeting. This made me feel more powerful with Larry, and with the board."

By changing how she responded to Larry's needling, Teresa was able to change her experience, which made it easier to respond in a way that served her when Larry started in. This is why alternative scenarios can be so useful: they enable us to move beyond our stock responses, which get activated by past experience. Changing the narrative gives us the power to challenge the automatic character of our triggered reactions. Instead, we create an environment that helps us to change and grow.

CAVEAT

Preparing ourselves to address triggers rather than letting them ambush and undermine us is one of the most important things we can do—for ourselves, our careers, our teams, our organizations, and our families. It can make us stronger and more clear-headed. It can help us engage allies based on our ability to take positive action, rather than looking for buddies to vent with. It can increase our self-respect and enable us to show up as a professionals in challenging circumstances. Ultimately, it can demonstrate that we are ready to take on bigger roles—as leaders, mentors, and valued colleagues.

I've outlined a few techniques for defusing triggers in this chapter and will be offering more throughout this book. They can be useful in many contexts, but are especially so in situations where gender, racial, ethnic, age, and sexual orientation divides provoke volatile emotions. In the chapters that follow, we will look at how the most common of these triggers operate and how we can defuse them and turn them to our advantage.

But first, an important caveat.

I am not recommending that the techniques in this book be used to confront truly toxic cultural behaviors, such as deliberate or ongoing harassment, clear or veiled threats, or instances or patterns of physical, psychological, or sexual abuse. Such tools as alternative scripts are neither appropriate nor effective against abusers, who tend to up the ante as a way of maintaining control. Attempting to defuse abusive situations does not set us on a more productive path. It may simply postpone a more extreme assault.

Abuse is not only a threat to those being abused but also to the entire system. As such, it needs to be addressed through channels that have structural authority over the abuser and the resources to rain down consequences. These include HR and legal professionals and, ultimately, the justice system. Such redress lies beyond the scope of this book.

Nor are techniques for addressing behavioral triggers the right tool for confronting systemic inequities with regard to hiring, promotion, or fair payment that continue to persist in organizations. These also require a systemic response that may involve collective or legal action, and benefit from securing professional support.

What I'm trying to provide in this book are imaginative yet proven ways to confront the kind of routine and common provocations that are not abusive but can nevertheless poison workplace relationships and diminish our ability to be happy and effective. It does us no good to suppress feelings that these everyday triggers stir or resort to trashing whoever provoked them. Nor are we served by overreacting and bringing in the big guns (*I'm filing a complaint with HR! I'm calling my lawyer!*) in situations that do not warrant it. Or by going public on Twitter.

For the truth is that such responses often backfire. Taking it to the wall, even when justified, may affect our reputation, expose us to public scrutiny, invite social media brutality, and put a torch to our careers. By contrast, being able to identify and confront common yet painful triggers provides a constructive means for addressing situations that may be infuriating but do not qualify as abusive.

CHAPTER TWO

Trigger 1: Visibility

We rise together by claiming visibility while
acknowledging the contributions of others

Successful careers are usually built on three legs: expertise, connections, and visibility. Of these, visibility is the least acknowledged.

We all know that we must master the skills required to do our jobs well, even exceptionally. And we've gotten the message that cultivating a strong network of support is essential. But rarely does anyone tell us that we need an intentional plan for getting recognized for our contributions, even though doing so does not come easily to many of us.

This is why visibility qualifies as a trigger. Since we're often operating based on insufficient information, we start to form our own ideas about why visibility is or is not important, as well as judgments about whether it should or should not matter. And it's these judgments that are likely to set us off.

In my experience, the trigger of visibility operates in three distinct though related ways. Let's look at each of them in turn.

WE FEEL TRIGGERED BY OUR
OWN LACK OF VISIBILITY

We work hard, show up, do our jobs conscientiously. We put effort into being a reliable colleague and a solid performer. Yet we often feel as if our hard work goes unnoticed and unrewarded. The promotion we believe we were due goes to a peer less skilled than we are. When company leaders talk about high potentials—*hi po's* (we hate that term)—our names never make the list. Even those who value our work don't seem to recognize what we could do if given half a chance.

We tell ourselves we shouldn't care, and try to take solace in our actual performance. And we put extra effort into continuing to hone our skills. But over time, we come to feel chronically underrecognized and undervalued, which can cause us to disengage from the job we've worked so hard to excel at. We start to wonder whether we're with the right company or in the right position. Despite our diligence, we can't seem to get traction. Maybe it's time to move on.

Moving on may or may not be a good idea, but one thing is sure. If we don't have a plan for getting recognized at our next job, we'll find ourselves in the same situation. That's because the responsibility for assuring that our contributions get noticed lies with us.

WE FEEL TRIGGERED BY COLLEAGUES
WHO ARE GOOD AT GETTING NOTICED

When our lack of visibility triggers us, we usually react in one of two ways. We may feel bad about ourselves or our job and end up losing hope, as described above. Or we may turn our resentment outward, toward those who seem effortlessly able to engage attention.

This is very common. In fact, one of the most frequent questions I'm asked in my workshops is:

"How can I bring attention to my achievements without acting like that jerk on my team?"

"Why is he a jerk?" I ask.

"He's a showboat, really full of himself. With him, it's all about *me*. The terrible thing is, it seems to work. He's viewed as a hotshot. But I'd rather stay below the radar than to be like him."

This questioner has put herself in a classic either/or bind. Either she keeps doing what isn't working for her while trying to take satisfaction in being a worthy and self-effacing person (so much nicer than that showboat on her team). Or she tries to copy the behavior of a colleague she disdains.

She's backed herself into this corner because her resentment over not being noticed has made her judgmental. Maybe the guy on her team *is* a jerk, but the fact remains that he's exercising a skill she's neglected to master. If she were less dismissive, she could apply her energy to studying what he does and adapting it to suit her own style.

- When he says, "I had the client eating out of my hand," she might say, "I felt a real bond with this client."
- When he notes, "Everyone said I did a great job," she might say, "The response to my efforts was gratifying."
- When he claims, "I got stellar results," she might say, "Our team scored a big win on this project. I was able to contribute by bringing in our Chicago client."

Moderating her colleague's brash style while being clear about what she has to offer could benefit this questioner in many ways. It would enable her to secure credit for her achievements in a way she feels comfortable with. It would move her beyond either/or thinking. And it could tame her resentment of colleagues who put in the effort required to get recognized for their contributions.

I call this technique interpersonal aikido.

In aikido, you use your opponent's body weight against them, letting them step into you while you gracefully move aside. The purpose of this subtle maneuver is to keep your opponent off balance, while you remain firmly rooted so you can proceed from a place of strength.

The example about "the jerk" illustrates this approach in very concrete terms. By demonstrating a more generous way of claiming visibility, the woman in question could give her male colleague a perfect opportunity to highlight the self-centered nature of his own approach. Then, instead of rushing to judgment, she could simply step aside and let others contrast her approach with his.

In politics, this is known as giving your opponent plenty of rope with which to hang themselves.

WE FEEL TRIGGERED BY PEOPLE WHO STRUGGLE WITH VISIBILITY

If we have a talent for promoting ourselves, we may feel triggered by those who refuse to do so, dismissing them as drudges, workhorses lacking in flair. Or we may decide that they are snobs who consider playing the games necessary for advancement to be beneath them.

Such judgments may inspire us take a Darwinian approach. As one executive I worked with declared, "It's sink or swim around here. If you can't speak up for yourself, if you can't figure out how to get yourself noticed, it's not my job to bring you into the spotlight."

Taking satisfaction in our own talent for visibility can make it hard to empathize with those who struggle. We fail to recognize the value introverted personalities contribute. We ignore the fact that those from outside the dominant group often have a history of getting shut down when they try to be assertive. Or, taking pride in our own star status, we may dismiss the skills others bring to the table as "mere competence." This can erode our commitment to putting in the hard work our jobs require and inspire us to blow things off, figuring that other people can take care of the details.

Despite our talents, those we work with begin to view us as jerks.

THE PERILS OF CONFIRMATION BIAS

These three visibility triggers, ostensibly so different, share some important common ground.

First, each leads us to overvalue one of the three legs on which a successful career is built:

- Being triggered by our lack of visibility can cause us to overvalue expertise.
- Being triggered by those who are good at compelling notice can cause us to overinvest in building connections, but in a negative way; if we're mentally tearing someone down, we may seek to bond with others who share our scorn.
- Being triggered by those who struggle to be visible can cause us to undervalue expertise, a common pitfall among high flyers and a frequent cause of their eventually flaming out.

Each of these responses also keeps us invested in self-serving narratives. We tell ourselves a story about why *our* approach is superior: how it makes us a better worker, or a nicer person, or proves that we have a more realistic understanding of what's required to get ahead. These self-vindicating tales don't make us terrible people. They simply show that we're human, prone to commending our own beliefs and talents in an effort to justify our own approach.

These stories also provide a perfect example of what behavioral scientists call the confirmation bias. This is the process by which our brains scan the environment in search of evidence that supports what we already believe, while filtering out information that might support other views.

A more useful approach than buying into the convenient narratives that run through our heads is to recognize them as cues that let us know we're being triggered. For that is precisely the information they convey. Whenever we hear ourselves saying, or even thinking,

"*I* would never . . . " or "*I'm* not the sort of person who . . . " in reference to someone else's behavior, we can be assured that their behavior is triggering us.

As noted in Chapter 1, this is an ideal moment to pause and tweak our internal dialogue. *Oh! I see, I'm being triggered. Maybe I need to question my usual story. Perhaps there's something I can learn here.*

NAVIGATING VISIBILITY TRIGGERS

Decades of watching people around the globe navigate visibility triggers has persuaded me that a few simple practices can help anyone assert their right to be noticed in a balanced and healthy way without getting dragged into the kind of self-congratulatory justifications that come so easily when we're on the defensive.

The simple practice of interpersonal aikido, as described earlier, can be hugely helpful. Other practices include:

- Claiming our space
- Extending interpersonal aikido
- Joining the fray
- Sharing the spotlight

All are especially useful when navigating gender, ethnic, and age divides—situations in which our confirmation bias often operates on high alert.

CLAIMING OUR SPACE

The road to visibility starts with the simple assertion of our presence. In any situation, no matter how awkward or disrespected we might feel, we declare with our hearts, our minds, and our bodies: *I am here; I have the right to be where and who I am. And I have the right to be acknowledged.*

This is the most basic level of visibility. And it is often where we need to start.

During Colonel Diane Ryan's twenty-nine-year career as an officer in the US Army, she served combat deployments in Operations Desert Storm and Iraqi Freedom. Following a string of general staff appointments, she spent nine years on the Department of Behavioral Sciences and Leadership faculty at the US Military Academy at West Point, finishing as academy professor, director of the Eisenhower Leader Development Program, and deputy department head. Yet despite her stellar career, Diane struggled throughout her years of service to have her presence acknowledged in the most basic way.

Diane says, "In the military, the issue of visibility is core and plays out every day. For example, people are supposed to acknowledge and salute anyone of superior rank every time they see them. Yet almost until the day I retired, men would routinely go out of their way to not see me. Because I was a woman who outranked them, they didn't want to concede my status. So they tried to ignore my presence."

Diane knew early on that she could not let this happen.

"Saluting a senior officer is a practice that has existed in the military going back to the days of knights in armor, so I could not let it go. Every time a man tried it, I forced myself to look directly at him and say simply but very firmly: *'Hello! Maybe you didn't see me?'* Even when it seemed obvious that the guy was doing everything possible to avoid me, I would give him the benefit of the doubt. I saw no sense in trying to humiliate him, which would only up the ante. But I always held my ground."

Similarly, male soldiers who did salute Diane would sometimes address her as "Sir." As in *"Hello, Sir."* "The implication was that I had to be a man if I outranked them because no woman possibly could. Again, even when I felt sure this was intentional, I would give them the benefit of the doubt by just correcting them, saying *'ma'am'* in a strong clear voice. Often, they'd offer some excuse: 'Oh, I didn't see you, I wasn't paying attention.' Okay, whatever. I would accept that with a nod and continue on."

Diane was inspired to stick with this effort by a senior officer early in her career who told her, "The standard you walk by is the standard you set." In other words, if you let something go—if you simply walk by it—you establish that as a baseline for what is acceptable. This is how misbehavior and microaggressions become entrenched. While you are not responsible for someone else's refusal to acknowledge you, you are responsible for holding them to account.

Diane did sometimes wonder whether extending the benefit of the doubt to enlistees and fellow officers intent on showing initial disrespect constituted a kind of pleasing behavior. But she maintained her approach because it was so effective. She knew from experience that triggers can blow up quickly and believed that defusing them was usually her best first line of defense. Her method combined strength with grace, which is what giving someone the benefit of the doubt amounts to. Grace is grace precisely because it is unearned yet freely given.

So Diane kept her focus on setting a standard by *not walking by*.

EXTENDING INTERPERSONAL AIKIDO

Claiming our space is not just a challenge for women. Culture can play a big role. Joohan, the chief technology officer in a fast-growth San Jose start-up, was born into a Korean family that valued self-effacement and modest behavior along with deference to anyone in authority. Joohan was also quiet and introverted, in contrast to his company's founder, Jay, a charismatic and supersmart boot-wearing Texan. Jay was a skilled promoter of the company and himself, a force of nature who knew how to grab attention.

Despite being opposites, Joohan and Jay made a strong team—except when meeting with investors. Jay needed Joohan at these meetings so he could answer the complex technical questions that potential venture funders were always throwing Jay's way. Yet despite his solid expertise, Joohan's discomfort in these meetings was palpable. He hated having the spotlight turned on him and responded by lowering his glance, but his hesitancy aroused Jay's natural impatience. Jay would refer a question to Joohan, but when Joohan didn't immediately respond, he would quickly cut him off. Accustomed to deferring to Jay as founder and unwilling to confront him, Joohan would then simply shut down.

Joohan felt the only solution was for Jay to somehow curb his impatience. But despite repeated requests, and despite their making a hash of several venture pitches, Jay proved incapable of sitting by while Joohan struggled to speak up.

Joohan's coach suggested he work on his body language as a way of making his presence felt, inhabiting his physical space in a more assertive way instead of trying fruitlessly to grab air time from Jay. At the time, Joohan was being treated for a back problem, so his coach suggested an unorthodox tactic. When he and Jay arrived for a pitch, Joohan would immediately announce that his chiropractor had told him he needed to stand during meetings. So while everyone settled into their places, Joohan would remain upright, focusing his attention on maintaining good posture.

The impact was immediate.

Joohan describes it. "Everyone had to look up at me and somehow that made a difference, as if I suddenly had more authority than I did when sitting down. I'd always thought my whole value was as a technical expert, but now I saw things weren't so simple. The first time Jay cut me off, he caught himself halfway through and actually apologized—I couldn't believe it. The second time, I heard myself say, 'I'm not quite finished,' and he backed right off. After a couple of meetings, Jay started standing when *he* had something to say. But it made us seem like pop-ups in a cartoon and he gave it up."

Standing in pitch meetings changed Joohan's view of his relationship with Jay. "I began having this image of myself as Jay's classroom teacher, and he was this restless little boy—charming and smart but ultimately not in control. Maybe it sounds silly, but this was good for me because it meant I was seeing Jay as a fellow human rather than a boss who could not be contradicted. That's so different from the hierarchical way my family taught me to view the world."

Joohan's experience taught him the value of asserting power in a physical way before trying to claim it verbally. As numerous researchers have found, assuming an authoritative stance signals our brains that we have the right to be where we are. It also cues others that we merit attention.

Acting as if we believe we have the right to claim visibility is a perfect example of the old adage *Fake it 'til you make it*. Simple as it is, asserting this right either verbally (like Diane) or physically (like Joohan) usually works.

Sun Tzu, the putative author of the ancient Chinese military treatise known as *The Art of War*, taught that using indirection or redirection to disarm an opponent is preferable to the direct engagement of combat—less costly and ultimately more effective. Again, both Diane Ryan and Joohan demonstrate the power of Sun Tzu's approach. Each used a variation of interpersonal aikido to compel recalcitrant or impatient colleagues to confirm their right to occupy their space.

Diane's commitment to giving antagonists the benefit of the doubt is also the equivalent of Sun Tzu's practice of "taking whole"—conquering an adversary in a way that preserves our own resources while enabling our opponent to retain a measure of dignity. We'll be looking at ways to apply this principle throughout this book, since such restraint is, as Sun Tzu also taught, key to creating ground from which we can rise together.

Even with those who may have treated us like opponents.

JOINING THE FRAY

When I speak before large groups of women, the questions come thick and fast. But if men are present, the women frequently clam up. In a 20 percent male audience, men will often pose half of the questions. If the audience is 40 percent male, only a few women may engage. This is especially true if the men hold senior positions.

Now, I don't believe that men are more fascinated by every word that drops from my lips than women, especially since women routinely waylay me after a talk to pose questions or share their responses. Rather, I view men's willingness to speak up as essentially strategic, a way of positioning themselves as contributors or players by joining the fray. An opportunity to claim recognition and get noticed.

Speaking up in a public setting is also an effective way to attract allies. For example, after I finish a keynote, both women and men will approach those who have commented, usually to support them ("That was a great question!") or to open a dialogue ("I love the point you made. I'm going to email you with some follow-up ideas."). This enables anyone who speaks up to organically extend their networks, further strengthening their visibility.

What happens in public forums also occurs in internal meetings, both in-person and virtual. For example, a global financial services company I worked with found a lack of visibility to be *the* chief impediment among their female managers, the key reason these women struggled to position themselves for promotion. I spoke briefly with the HR lead who'd developed the data. "It's hardly a surprise," he said. "We have a huge problem getting women to speak in meetings, which tend to be dominated by men. The upshot is that talented women stay below the radar."

When I interviewed the women in the company, some explained that they didn't like to speak before they had every fact nailed down. Others noted that they "wanted to make sure other people got a chance to talk." Many reported that when they'd spoken up in the past, no one had responded. "It kept happening," said one, "so I just gave up."

I hear some variation on these remarks all the time. Many cultures make it difficult for women, or other perceived outsiders, to speak up. Those who do may get tagged as arrogant or self-serving. So it's not surprising that, in an effort to be accommodating or avoid being seen as troublemakers, those who fear being described this way choose to remain silent.

Yet the willingness of women and other outsiders to "walk by" does set a standard that can make it hard for others to engage. As Melicia, a self-assured marketing director at the financial services company cited earlier, told me, "I hate being the only woman who routinely speaks in meetings. The other women tell me how brave I am. But I always want to ask, what are you afraid of?"

Of course, it's not just women who struggle in these situations. Introverted men, or indeed anyone from a culture that prizes deference or has been viewed as outside the leadership mainstream, are likely to do so, as we saw with Joohan. Yet the issue is less *who* struggles than *how* to address it, especially since the virtual workplace makes speaking up both harder and more essential.

Three simple practices can help those who are hesitant to join the fray.

Preparing

We often assume that people who speak confidently in public settings or pose clear questions are naturally self-assured, born with a certain talent or an innate self-confidence. But the truth is that people who do so usually make a habit of being well prepared. They review the topic under discussion in advance and decide on the points they'd like to raise if they get the chance. And they think through how they might best phrase their remarks, questions, or comments.

I once asked Sherry, the highest-ranking woman at a global bio-tech firm, what she viewed as the chief reason for her meteoric rise (we'll hear more from Sherry in Chapter 5). Without hesitation, she cited her ability to speak clearly and concisely in meetings or when making a presentation to the executive team. She said, "It's an invalu-able skill but it's not one you're born with. It requires a lot of prepara-tion. You make notes, you work on your phrasing. You rehearse what you want to say in advance. People think it's all very spontaneous, but it's not. You have to put in some work, but the rewards can be out of proportion to the effort."

Speaking up is in itself a form of preparation, which means we get better as we practice. We discover what lines work, what thoughts resonate, what gets a laugh. Speaking aloud also helps us clarify our thoughts, so we can better convey our meaning the next time we speak.

Anyone who has ever been on a book tour can affirm this.

At first, despite having spent a few years thinking about our sub-ject, we stumble to express ourselves or simply ramble. But after be-ing interviewed a few dozen times, we get our footing. Soon we know just what to say, and how to frame it smoothly and concisely. We make rapid progress because we have so many opportunities to hone our message.

Enlisting

Those who struggle to speak up can also benefit from enlisting sup-port in advance. We simply let a few people know that we're plan-ning to make a few comments if the moment is right. And we ask their advice.

For example, we might say, "Can I get your help? Tomorrow's meeting has made me nervous in the past so I've mostly kept quiet. But we're going to be looking at the new business plan, and I have a few ideas about how we might improve it. Can I take a minute to run what I want to say by you?"

Or we might say, "I know you're going to be at the brainstorming session next week. I'm planning to share a few ideas, which can be hard for me. If what I say resonates, would you mind saying so in the meeting? I've noticed that my comments often get lost in the shuffle so it would be great to have support."

This technique has several advantages:

- It gives us a jump start on the process of speaking up, which makes it easier to do so in the actual meeting.
- Bailing at the last moment feels like less of an option when we've made a point of telling someone else that we plan to speak.
- Asking for support helps us extend and broaden our network, reaching beyond the usual suspects.

The key to this kind of informal enlistment is limiting requests to a specific time and a specific meeting, rather than issuing a vague plea for help. Thinking ahead about how we might frame our request serves as an additional form of preparation, yet another a chance to practice speaking up.

Centering

When we're nervous, our tendency is to speak too quickly, plunging in headlong and letting the words rush out. This increases the likelihood of losing our train of thought or forgetting to make an essential point. The stress we convey can also make it difficult for others to hear us because they feel the effect of our nervous tension.

To combat this, it's good to get into the habit of centering ourselves before we speak. The easiest way to do so is to take a few slow, deep breaths before we say anything. This is effective because it clears our minds and banishes distraction, enabling us to be present for what we want to say and for those we want to hear us. Slowing our breath also diminishes our stress by signaling to our nervous system that we are relaxed. If you're skeptical, try taking three deep breaths while worrying about something else. It doesn't work because breathing connects you to the here and now.

By contrast, failing to be fully present when we are speaking undermines our capacity to have an impact because people can read that our minds are somewhere else. And if we're not engaged, why should *they* listen? Again, if you're skeptical, please consider that a baby can tell when you're distracted—try calming an infant when you're on the phone. A dog can tell—try training one while chatting with a friend. A horse can tell—try keeping your mount while stewing over what someone just said.

If a baby, a dog, or a horse can read our distraction, why would a roomful of colleagues be any different?

SHARING THE SPOTLIGHT

Just as creating a culture of visibility requires those who prefer not to speak up to share their thoughts, so it also requires that those who enjoy engaging turn the spotlight on others. Offering verbal encouragement and support to colleagues or team members in the habit of holding back can benefit our teams and organizations, earn us a substantial amount of good will, burnish our reputations, and even change the course of our careers.

Roger had just retired as COO of a major telecom company when I met him at an industry retreat in Dubai. By chance, I had read an article about him in an inflight business magazine that lauded his reputation as a world-class champion for female talent. He personally had mentored three women who had gone on to assume C-suite positions in global firms.

Over lunch, I asked Roger what made him such an effective advocate for women. He surprised me by saying he'd earned the reputation accidentally.

"It all started when I was leading a big cable rollout that had turned into a world-class mess," he said. "I called a meeting of my senior people plus a few of our technical staff to see if we could come up with any solutions. The idea was to do a group brainstorm, the blue-sky approach, everyone just throwing out ideas."

Roger went around the room, asking participants for ideas, but nothing of much value was put forth. Then he called on Carlene, who was relatively junior. He says, "I barely knew her—she didn't speak much. But it turned out that she'd worked on an undersea cable task force when she was in the navy and had some great suggestions about how we could change our approach."

When Carlene finished sharing what she knew, Roger asked for comments from the room. "I figured most people would see the value in what she had said. But the guys either totally ignored her or started in on all the reasons why what she'd suggested couldn't possibly work. Which is not what blue sky is supposed to be about."

After a few go-rounds, Roger brought the meeting to a close by saying that, unless someone had a better idea, the team would test out Carlene's suggestion.

"Then one of the guys in the room started snickering and said, 'Oh, I see. Now we're being politically correct.'

"I couldn't believe it. I told him, 'Well, maybe I missed it when you told us your better idea. Would you like to share that with us now?'

"The guy looked mortified, and I thought, what the hell, but I was really shocked. We were supposed to be operating on this 'one team' idea but clearly a few of the guys hadn't gotten the memo."

After the meeting, Carlene approached Roger to thank him for supporting her in such a public way. "That's the fifth time I've spoken in that meeting," she said, "but the first time anyone seemed to hear me. I'm very grateful you handled it like you did."

As it turned out, Carlene's suggestion was the first step in resolving the impasse, and the cable initiative moved forward to become a big success. But the incident in the blue-sky meeting also had a big impact. To Roger's surprise, word of his intervention spread like wildfire. "Within forty-eight hours, it seemed as if every single woman in our ninety-thousand-person global workforce had heard how I'd spoken up for Carlene," he told me. "Overnight, I got this reputation as a huge supporter of women. Women started applying to be in my unit, saying they wanted to work for me. All because I had stood up in that meeting and endorsed Carlene's suggestion."

The incident turned out to be a huge plus for Roger given that, a few years later, the company undertook a high-profile effort to become the employer of choice for women. He was asked to speak at the company's first-ever women's leadership conference and some of the most talented women in the company sought him out as a mentor.

As women rose in the company, so did Roger. Putting the spotlight on Carlene turned out to be one of the best career moves he ever made.

CHAPTER THREE

Trigger 2: Managing Perceptions

*We rise together by neither over- nor
undermanaging what others think*

Perhaps the most frequent question I get from women during my workshops is some variation on the following:

"How can I represent my achievements/claim credit for my successes without anyone thinking I'm self-centered/aggressive/too ambitious?"

I have never heard this question from a man.

Let's forget that the women who ask this have signed up for a leadership program, and so might be presumed to have some level of ambition. And that most of them probably know from experience that being intentional in the pursuit of their goals (as good a definition of ambition as any) has been essential in shaping their accomplishments so far.

It's being *perceived* as ambitious—or aggressive, or self-centered—that they fear. Often to an extent that contradicts what they've actually achieved.

Think about that phrasing: "without anyone thinking . . . "

Anyone? Really? Is this even possible? And why is what "anyone" thinks so important?

Psychiatrist Anna Fels, in her landmark book *Necessary Dreams*, noted that senior female partners in top-rated New York law firms and investment banks, a key part of her clientele, often started their first visit by informing her that they were "not ambitious." They had simply worked hard and been very lucky.

Now, anyone who has spent five minutes in one of these cultures recognizes this as a doubtful proposition. These tough, star-centric environments both require and reward ambition. You don't make partner without wanting it badly, positioning yourself skillfully, and working like a demon for egregiously long hours. Even getting hired at one of these firms requires fierce dedication, a degree of competitive aggression, and commitment to making sacrifices in pursuit of a goal.

Yet these extraordinarily successful women were so triggered by the fear of anyone thinking they were ambitious that they tried to deny it even to their psychiatrist!

Of course, a lot has changed since 2004, when Anna's book was published, including the MeToo movement and a cascade of firsts for women leaders. So I decided to ask Anna whether her findings still held true.

Fortunately, she reported that the situation has changed for many, though not all, of her clients. "Among the younger women, ambition is no longer a Scarlet Letter word," she said. But she emphasized that her direct experience lay mostly among superhigh achievers in sophisticated New York City–based firms. "I'm not sure if it's all that different in other parts of the country, or the world."

I'm here to say that progress on this front remains uneven.

In many organizations, especially those outside major metropolitan areas, as well as in cultures that have traditionally placed a high value on female self-effacement, women and other outsiders to the leadership mainstream still report fearing that being seen as too assertive or ambitious will put them on a fast track to a poor reputation. The upshot is that they spend a lot of energy on trying to manage other people's perceptions.

Those in the dominant group can also be triggered into trying to manage others' perceptions, but it manifests differently and is spurred by different concerns, as we shall see later in this chapter. Understanding how these two ends of the perception spectrum operate, and the consequences they have for us and for those we work with, can help us consign concerns about "what people think" to their proper place.

THE DOUBLE BIND

The reason perception triggers operate differently is not far to seek. For the truth is that women, as well as people of color, are likely to have been criticized for behaviors that are routinely accepted from men in the dominant group.

This disparity has become known as the double bind, a damned-if-you-do-damned-if-you-don't trap that offers no intuitive way out.

- You're viewed as lacking impact and leadership potential if you don't speak up strongly and clearly . . .
  . . . but you're deemed overbearing if you do.
- You're judged as hyperpolitical if you try to build relationships that enhance your access and build your position . . .
  . . . but you're dismissed as "not a player" if you fail to do so.
- You're seen as not being a team player if you talk about your individual contributions . . .
  . . . but you're routinely overlooked when it comes time for promotions because people don't know what you've accomplished.

Research confirms that the double bind is pervasive. Multiple studies note that while being viewed as assertive and ambitious marks men as potential leaders, these same attributes are often perceived as negatives in women, arousing old stereotypes about women being shrill and bossy. And while the ability to show emotion is often regarded as proof of a man's passion and commitment, women who stand strongly behind their beliefs or ideas are typically deemed "too emotional."

Women I work with offer baroque twists on how the double bind plays out in their own work lives.

From an aerospace engineer in the U.S. defense industry:

I contradicted a colleague in a meeting when he misrepresented some data I had developed. Our team leader told me on the spot that I'd spoken out of turn. Afterward, he continued to chastise me for undermining team harmony. He even dragged out that old cliché about how "there is no *i* in team." I found this obnoxious because the whole meeting had been contentious, with several of the guys challenging the hell out of one another. The tone didn't seem to bother our team leader until I made my objection. I guess he couldn't handle even a fact-based challenge if it came from a woman.

From an associate in a Swedish law firm:

I was asked to contribute to a client presentation. I know the client has a short attention span, so I really prepared to be concise. My segment was the shortest one that day by almost fifteen minutes. Nevertheless, at the dinner afterward, several of my male colleagues began teasing me about how I had gone on and on. One said, "You sounded like my wife when I ask, 'How was your day?' I get this whole litany when 'fine' would have been enough."

From a communications manager in a UK transport company whose family had emigrated from the Caribbean:

> I asked one of our executives in a town hall to clarify a point by offering an example. Two people came up to me afterward and said, "You seem pretty angry." I get that a lot—the angry Black woman thing. If I challenge anyone, people automatically assume I have a grievance, which they often seem to attribute to race. Most colleagues try to be subtle about this, but sometimes it's right out there.

WHAT WE CAN CONTROL

I had an opportunity to work with Simone, the manager trying to battle the "angry Black woman" tag.

After she'd described a number of experiences, I asked how she had been dealing with it.

She said, "Basically, I put a lot of effort into trying to show that I'm not an angry person. This means I sometimes don't speak up even when I know I should. It gets complicated when I assert myself, so I tend to avoid it. And I probably back down too easily. Sometimes I hear myself apologizing for things I didn't even say!"

How was this approach working for her?

"Well, on the plus side, I don't hear the angry charge as much as I used to. So in that way, I guess it's helpful. On the other hand, I'm trying so hard not to say anything that some coworkers or clients might see me as ineffective. So, I'm kind of disappearing into my job, instead of really putting myself out there."

I suggested that Simone consider whether she was privileging something she could not control (other people's perceptions) over something she could control, which was showing up fully for her job. Certainly, some of her coworkers were insensitive, stuck in outdated modes of thought. Maybe they hadn't had much experience working with people from different cultures. Or maybe they'd grown up in environments where bias was taken for granted.

Was there any action she could take that would change that?

"I've thought about it," she said. "But I don't see lodging a complaint because someone says, 'You seem angry.' I've also considered posting about it on social media, but a friend of mine went that route and it led to disaster. Of course, I *could* talk to HR about doing a workshop on stereotypes—that might be helpful. Probably some people here don't even know that 'angry Black woman' is a stereotype!"

After exploring the pros and cons of confrontation, Simone decided to investigate possible workshops she might recommend to her company. But her big takeaway was deciding to spend less of her energy focusing on what other people thought. She said, "Half the time, it's just ignorance. I guess the truth is, though I can play a role in changing the culture, I can't change it by myself. So holding back on what I have to contribute in hopes of proving that I'm not an angry person isn't really the way to go."

If Simone could free herself from the fear of being perceived as angry, how might she direct that energy?

"Focus on doing the best job I can without second-guessing. Not let stupid comments derail me. Build relationships that give people a chance to see who I am. Position myself to be better known for what I have to offer. Develop new skills. Speak up clearly when I have something important to say."

Of course, it's not *fair* that Simone should have to deal with this kind of backward behavior—a topic we'll explore at greater length in Chapter 6. But this is the situation in which she finds herself now. To address the culture in her 150-year-old British transport company, she probably needs to put herself in a more powerful position than the one she presently holds. And showing up more forcefully in her job rather than hiding her light under a barrel in an effort to avoid stereotyped misperceptions is a more likely course for attaining this kind of power—and blowing past the double bind.

As Michelle Obama said when confronted with the shopworn "angry Black woman" charge, "When they go low, I aim high." And part of aiming high is keeping our focus on what we can control.

North Carolina–based leadership coach Terry Jackson reports that Black men are also often perceived as angry.

"I see it with my clients, and I've experienced it myself when I was in corporate life," he says. "In one company, I had an African American male boss who saw me as enthusiastic and passionate. But then he moved up and a white man took his place. The first thing this guy said to me after a meeting was, 'You seem quite angry.' I concluded it was his problem, not mine, and didn't waste my time trying to prove him wrong."

WHAT DOES IT TAKE TO CHANGE SOMEONE'S MIND?

One reason trying to manage perceptions is problematic is that it deprives others of the chance to change their minds about us. In our anxiety to make sure that *no one* thinks we're too aggressive, too ambitious, too angry, or too . . . (fill in the dots), we forget that anyone who is not ideologically committed to a negative assessment may shift their opinion if we give them time.

I learned this early in my career, when I worked in corporate communications. One day in a meeting, I was the only woman present and the most junior person in the room, so I was feeling a bit out of my depth. Yet because the topic under discussion was within my area of expertise, I found the nerve to raise my hand and offer an idea that I'd been noodling over.

No one responded. It was as if I hadn't spoken. An embarrassed hush settled over the room. It was broken only when one of the top dogs on the team made a suggestion that had nothing to do with what I had proposed. I felt deflated, though not especially surprised.

Then, as we were leaving the meeting, Fred, my boss's boss, sidled up behind me and murmured in a sarcastic tone: "Well! *You* certainly aren't afraid to share your opinion."

I was astonished. Fred had never spoken to me. Now I'd succeeded in getting on his bad side. I could hardly have felt more crushed. But for some reason, I did not respond in what was my usual way at the time.

I didn't apologize or grovel: "Oh, I'm so sorry, maybe I shouldn't have spoken . . . (*please forgive me, Your Highness*)."

Nor was I defensive: "I have a perfect right to speak my mind!"

Instead, I heard myself saying simply: "No, I'm not."

As Fred harrumphed away, I thought, *Well, I'm cooked. My boss's boss thinks I'm out of line.* I figured I'd better start looking for another job since I was clearly going nowhere in this company.

But nothing happened. Time passed. I sat in on some more meetings where Fred was present and made a few contributions when I had something to say. After all, I had nothing to lose. Since I was probably going to be leaving anyway, why should I shut myself down?

Then one day, a month or two later, I happened to be walking down the hall when I overheard Fred speaking to a colleague in an adjoining room.

"You know what I like about Sally?" he was saying. "She's not afraid to speak her mind."

I could hardly believe my ears. He seemed to approve of the very quality he had criticized me for so harshly.

It took me a while to understand what had happened. Because I had replied to his putdown in a neutral way and persevered instead of swooping in to try to manage what he thought, I'd given him time and space to get to get used to me and adjust his assessment.

As a result, I'd been able to secure his good opinion on *my* terms. All it took was a little time. And sufficient discipline to refrain from trying to manage Fred's perceptions.

ONE OF THE GOOD GUYS

As a rule, men in the dominant group don't need to struggle with the double bind. They're rarely critiqued for being ambitious or talking up their achievements, so that particular part of the damned-if-you-do equation does not apply. Of course, some men rigorously avoid anything that even suggests self-promotion. But this is often because they're introverts or were raised in deferential cultures. Even in female-dominated or -led organizations, male ambition and assertiveness tend to be accepted, viewed as proof of confidence or an enviable comfort with power.

But this doesn't mean that men don't wrestle with managing perceptions. As organizations grow more global and the workforce more diverse, the rules of engagement keep shifting. As a result, men's earnest efforts to be perceived in a positive light can go seriously awry, creating precisely the kind of backlash they hope to avoid.

I recently sat through a presentation by a health care chief executive officer widely considered to be an inclusive and inspiring leader. Arthur is known for having promoted many women to senior positions and for being an active champion of his company's diversity initiative. In his sector, and in the business press, he's viewed as one of the good guys.

Arthur's session, part of a large health care conference, was billed as a leadership keynote, meant to focus on the practices that had made him successful. He felt his usual ease when he arrived at the venue, but he was startled to find that the majority of his audience was female. Because his session was intended for the most senior people at the conference, he'd assumed he'd be speaking mostly to men.

Awaiting his turn at the podium, Arthur began to second-guess his prepared remarks. What if the women couldn't relate to his stories? Or what if they viewed leadership as a male-centric topic? He remembered having read something about that. At the last minute, he decided to refocus his talk. Having nothing specific in mind, Arthur found himself spending a good amount of his time onstage talking about his wife.

He spoke about how brilliant she was. He praised her insight and her good judgment. He noted that he asked her advice whenever he had to make an important decision and confessed that she was actually a better leader than he was and should probably be standing up here instead of him. The only reason she was not, he said, was that she "had made the choice to stay at home with our children."

It was clear that Arthur had decided the best way to connect with his heavily female audience was by extravagantly praising the woman he knew best. This of course raised a couple of questions. Why at this point in history (it was early 2020, just before in-person events shut down) did he not recognize that a leadership session *in the health care sector* might attract a lot, even a preponderance, of women? And why did he assume that having women in the audience required him to adjust his remarks?

I wondered whether the female participants in his session were as surprised as I was. So during the lunch that followed, I informally polled as many of them as I could.

Their impressions were scathing.

"I guess he talks to women so rarely that he has no idea what to say."

"He sounded as if his wife is the only woman he knows, which is unfortunate because he's got a good reputation."

"I found him incredibly condescending. All that stuff about how smart his wife is. Does he think that's so amazing in a woman?"

"That line about his wife 'choosing' to stay home with the kids: was that his way of telling us *we're* not good mothers? Whatever he intended, he made it clear what he thinks of women who actively pursue their careers. Which of course included most of the women in his audience!"

For balance, I asked a male colleague for his impressions. "Well," he said, "I assumed Arthur was adjusting his content because there were so many women at the conference. But I bet the women loved hearing him talk about his wife."

Not so much.

In truth, Arthur's reluctance to discuss leadership given the presence of so many women ended up alienating a good part of his audience. Despite his good intentions, his obvious surprise made him seem both entitled and clueless about who was sitting in the room.

It also made him seem old, especially to the millennials present, male as well as female. The 1950s sitcom lifestyle he was describing— wise wife at home, bumbling husband bringing home the bacon— not surprisingly struck them as out of date.

To his credit, Arthur recognized that things had not gone well, and asked a female coach for help. She suggested that, going forward, he assume that any conference or even meeting he spoke at would have a significant number of women in attendance. And that they would be interested in the same kind of insights as men.

The coach also recommended that Arthur make a practice of running his remarks by a few women in advance of delivering an important talk. She noted that if he had previewed the talk he ended up delivering to a female colleague, she most likely would have said, "Do not talk about how wonderful your wife is. Men do that all the time. To most women, it feels like pandering. Also, the way you're doing it is insulting. You clearly have a built-in support system that frees you from having to worry about whatever is happening at home. Most of the women in your audience do not. So you're basically chastising them for providing essential support for their families while rubbing their faces in the fact that their families enjoy less privilege than yours."

NOT-SO-GOOD GUY BEHAVIORS

Arthur was able to shift his approach because he viewed becoming more skilled at addressing female audiences as essential to his reputation as a leader. But not all men in senior positions are so willing to adapt. They may resent the idea of having to manage perceptions, believing it lies outside their job description. Or they may view a refusal to adjust as proof of their integrity and toughness.

Amsterdam-based leadership coach and author Jeffrey Hull describes working with male clients who become frustrated when he even suggests they become more aware of how they come across. He says, "Some of these guys are used to not caring what anyone thinks. They've been very successful and don't believe they should spend time or energy adjusting to a changing environment. They tell me, 'I know I'm *supposed* to be all touchy-feeling and develop these soft skills because there are all kinds of people in the workplace these days. But basically, I think it's a fad. It's being PC. And I'm not buying in.'"

Jeff observes that men with this attitude often view becoming more flexible as letting someone else—women and/or minorities—dictate the terms of their engagement. "These guys tend to be highly competitive, which means they try to score a win off every encounter. If they don't come out on top, it feels like a loss. Plus they know that women often excel at the kind of soft skills they lack. They don't want to concede that these skills have value because they fear that would give women an edge."

Jeff also notes that being more flexible would require these men to try out behaviors they rarely practice and so are not very good at. "Humility is not in their toolkit, so doing something differently makes them uncomfortable. This is natural—we all feel uncomfortable when we try something new. Nobody *likes* doing it, but it's how we grow and develop. Men stuck in this mind-set need to recognize that refusing to grow is an increasingly poor career move."

CIRCLE OF CONCERN, CIRCLE OF CONTROL

I've noted several times the importance of distinguishing between what concerns us and what we can control. The concept comes from Stephen Covey's mega-bestseller *The Seven Habits of Highly Effective People*. This landmark book drew from two divergent themes in self-help literature: the early twentieth-century focus on building character and the more recent focus on being successful, at work and in our communities.

Among the many helpful tools Covey introduced to readers was an illustration of two simple circles, which he labeled the circle of concern and the circle of influence. Inside our circle of concern are all the things we care about: our family, our colleagues and friends, our workplace, and the larger world. Inside our circle of influence are those things that lie within our control: the actions we take, the words we speak, how we respond to opportunities and setbacks.

Covey noted that when these two circles are out of alignment—when we are so concerned with what we can't control that we pay insufficient attention to what we can—we end up spinning our wheels, squandering mental and emotional energy. By contrast, the more our circles of concern and control overlap, the more "highly effective," and the happier, we will be.

Distinguishing where our circles do and do not overlap is especially helpful when it comes to managing perceptions for the simple reason that we cannot ultimately control what other people think. Simone at the UK transport company can tie herself into knots trying never to challenge any of her coworkers, but she cannot control those among them who are primed to equate any assertiveness in a Black woman with anger. She is therefore better off attending to those things she can control:

- Doing her best
- Doing what she can to assure that her contributions are noticed

- Providing honest feedback in a way that is helpful even when it may not be perceived as pleasing
- Maintaining the kind of enthusiastic but grounded demeanor that can sustain her through challenging times

Arthur too could have benefited from having a better alignment between his circle of concern and his circle of influence. Startled by the number of women in his audience, he could have decided on the spot to focus on what he could control: delivering his prepared talk smoothly and powerfully, with humility and humor. Instead, he focused his efforts on trying to assure that his female listeners would view him as one of the good guys.

The truth is, what other people think of us is not usually any of our business. If a coworker chooses to resent us, so be it. Over time, he or she may reconsider, as my former boss's boss Fred did. But for the moment, we can't control it, so we need to let it go. Doing so requires discipline and detachment—admittedly, a tough order. But it offers us the most effective path through the treacheries of the double bind.

CHAPTER FOUR

Trigger 3: Confidence and Competence

We rise together by distinguishing
overconfidence from competence

The best story I know about confidence concerns Alan Mulally, former CEO of the Ford Motor Company, at one of his first meetings with the company's senior executive team. Based on Alan's reputation as a strong leader who excelled in getting people to work well together throughout his long career at Boeing, Bill Ford had recruited him to lead the company in 2006. This was unprecedented in a culture where being a lifelong "car guy" had traditionally been the highest accolade and primary proof of credibility. Every previous CEO in Ford's history had been a lifer in the company.

Mulally, by contrast, was a self-proclaimed airplane guy, who habitually signed his name with a Chinese pictogram of his face on a plane, drawn in his own hand. He had initially resisted accepting the top position in an organization known for assessing talent based on automotive knowledge and experience. But Bill Ford pushed hard, recognizing that the company's depth of knowledge had not been sufficient to prevent it from steadily losing market share and falling $18 billion into debt.

Alan's first meeting with the Ford executive team—the generals and the colonels, as they've always been known—had the potential to be fraught. And sure enough, shortly after introducing himself, and sharing his pictogram, Alan was asked a highly technical question calculated to test his car-guy chops.

The assembled leadership held its collective breath.

Alan thanked his questioner. Then he simply noted that, having come from outside the industry, he did not have the expertise to answer the question, reiterating that he had spent his career in aerospace.

One can imagine the shock. The newly appointed CEO of Henry Ford's world-transforming company was publicly admitting he couldn't answer a straightforward question because his background had not prepared him to do so.

Alan then pointed out that, although *he* couldn't answer, Ford was filled with brilliant and experienced automotive experts who could. His job was not to provide answers but to create an environment that enabled the team at Ford to identify and implement solutions that could return the company to profitability and greatness.

How many CEOs would acknowledge during their first meeting with their new company's leadership team that they didn't know the answer to a vital question because their experience hadn't qualified them to give one? And how many would say so plainly and clearly, without bluster or defensive pushback?

Yet Alan could answer this way because he had sufficient confidence to not be triggered into trying to demonstrate a competence he knew he did not possess. In addition:

- He understood that trying to earn respect based on qualifications he did not have was a losing game.

- He did not fear that demonstrating humility would result in him seeming weak.
- He knew he couldn't control what others thought (his circles of influence and concern were in alignment).
- He trusted that the experience he did have would get results.

RIGHT SIZING

Showing humility by honestly admitting our limitations and displaying a right-sized sense of who we are becomes more challenging as we move into higher or more visible positions. Given that our global business culture often expects leaders to be all-knowing heroes or saviors, we get the message that if we let any chinks in our armor show, others may perceive us as undeserving of the power with which we've been entrusted. As a result, we may become so fearful of appearing vulnerable or underqualified that we end up misrepresenting ourselves.

This is not only true at the leadership level. Many of us equate being humble with opening ourselves up to humiliation. And so we're tempted to pretend we have expertise that we lack.

Such responses do not serve us and are unlikely to yield positive results, in part because they undermine our ability to feel comfortable about ourselves. By contrast, Alan was confident that his well-honed ability to create a culture in which talented people could work creatively and collaboratively together could make him successful in the top job at Ford.

He also avoided falling prey to the common delusion that, because he had expertise in one domain, he was therefore an expert in everything else.

Coach Jeffrey Hull calls this "the fallacy of omnicompetence" and describes it as one of the most common hazards of outsized success. Says Hull, "People tend to extrapolate. They think, 'I'm a great ER doctor, so of course I can run this hospital. It's a no-brainer for someone with my skills.' They forget that their skills, while considerable, have almost nothing to do with the job they aspire to. Why? Because they have little sense of their own limitations."

This kind of I-have-all-the-skills mind-set shows a failure of self-awareness, adds Hull, noting that his job as a coach is to help clients view themselves more realistically. "They need to get comfortable letting others see them as who they are—skills, warts, flaws, strengths, the whole package. For this to happen, they need to accept the truth that excelling at one thing does not mean they will excel in another."

Concludes Hull, "Having the humility to accept this makes you more human, because you're showing vulnerability. You let go of the burden of trying to prove you're something you're not. People avoid doing this, but it usually comes as a huge relief—to them, and to everyone around them. Because those who lack humility do not inspire trust."

HAVING WHAT IT TAKES

When I tell the Ford story to groups of women, someone inevitably objects. "Okay, that's great for Alan Mulally. But he's a white American male engineer. He can afford to admit when he doesn't know the answer and talk about how he's an airplane guy in a company that manufactures cars. I'd like to see a woman try that. If she'd just been hired as a leader and she admitted she didn't know answers to questions people expected her to know, she'd be laughed out of her job."

There's no question that demonstrating Mulally-level self-assurance is easier for those in the dominant group—although it's also rare, which is why the Ford story is such a standout. Those who look like previous leaders tend to get the benefit of the doubt from colleagues and customers. Trust is often theirs to lose.

By contrast, if we're outsiders to the leadership mainstream, we've typically had to battle perceptions about whether we have what it takes—in performance reviews, evaluation meetings, and informal conversations.

For example:

- "I'm not convinced she has the temperament of a leader."
- "Are you sure he didn't get here as part of a diversity quota?"
- "My guess is she may have been held to a lower standard than some of our other candidates."
- "I know he has a PhD, but I'd like to see what kind of grade point average he had to qualify."

Given the prevalence of such condescending doubts, it's not surprising that women and people of color might be uncomfortable displaying any lack of expertise in high, or even low, stakes situations. A history of having to deal with negative perceptions makes it hard to manage the kind of ease and aplomb that Alan Mulally so compellingly displayed.

In addition, those from outside the dominant group often worry that fumbles on their part could make it harder for others in their cohort to rise. So failing to have all the answers may feel risky not only to themselves, but for those who come after them.

That's a lot of baggage to carry around.

LESSONS FROM AN ICEBREAKER

Yet there are ways that outsiders can gracefully claim authority without having to pretend they have all the answers. An example comes from Sandy Stosz, who retired out of the US Coast Guard (USCG) as vice admiral and the first woman ever to head a major service academy.

Sandy graduated from the US Coast Guard Academy she would later head in 1982, when women made up only 2 percent of the entire service. Given the numbers, as well as the USCG's proud male-dominated history and culture, it's not surprising that some senior leaders believed, and openly proclaimed, that a ship was no place for a woman.

Nevertheless, Sandy eagerly sought seagoing assignments and landed consecutive ensign positions aboard icebreakers, deploying to both Antarctica and the Arctic. Icebreakers are heavy cutters that clear channels through massive sheets of polar ice to enable the supply ships that support scientific and national security missions to get through.

As the first, and then one of only two women aboard these multi-month voyages, Sandy had to prove herself by building her skills, setting high performance goals for herself, being a reliable team member, and maintaining a professional demeanor in all circumstances. She learned, as she says, that "the best antidote to bias is demonstrating competence through performance and professional presence."

Her first command assignment was on the icebreaker *Katmai Bay*, homeported in Sault Sainte Marie, Michigan, and charged with clearing channels for the huge merchant vessels that plied the often-frozen Great Lakes and their surrounding rivers. At the time, no woman had ever commanded a Coast Guard ship on the Great Lakes, and her ship had an all-male crew. Shortly before taking this assignment, Sandy had served as an aide to the US secretary of transportation. When she learned that he would be attending the ceremony marking the ship's shift to her command, she was thrilled.

Given the presence of the Washington cabinet member responsible for the USCG, she assumed the Coast Guard brass would be eager to attend the ceremony, but the opposite proved to be true. Her new supervisor informed her on her first day of work that she was "nothing but the secretary's fair-haired golden girl," rather than the experienced icebreaker hand with multiple polar voyages to her credit she actually was. Her supervisor then went on to warn her that he'd be testing her on a daily basis to make sure she was up to the job, a proposition he clearly doubted and seemed eager to disprove.

His ongoing intimidation created a shipboard climate of unrest that Sandy attributed to the confusion caused by the crew seeing her do the right things even as she was being constantly called out by her supervisor. Yet despite the sniping, Sandy's confidence soared during her command. This happened for three reasons.

First, she had plenty of opportunities to test the competencies she'd worked so hard to develop on previous assignments, not only aboard icebreakers but running Coast Guard law enforcement and rescue missions that required finesse in volatile situations.

Second, she went out of her way to cultivate as shipboard allies anyone who seemed open to her as leader. She found particular support in the *Katmai Bay*'s chief petty officer, one of the most senior enlisted men on the ship. He advocated for her with the crew and even put his career on the line by pushing back against her supervisor on occasions when his harassment went over the top.

Third, Sandy was able to find her own distinctive voice as a leader because she remained willing to ask questions, despite having been advised that doing so would only highlight her female uncertainty and lack of suitability for command.

For example, she'd been warned in advance that the experienced merchant shipmasters who operated on the Great Lakes would never trust an icebreaker crew led by a woman. So shortly after taking charge, she contacted one of the big shipping firms to arrange a visit aboard one of their ore carriers. Meeting with its shipmaster, she asked him what she saw as the most vital question. Given that her vessel was 140 feet long and his was 1,000 feet long, what would be most helpful for her to know in advance about clearing a path that would help him navigate?

The master expressed astonishment. He told her that in all the decades he'd been piloting in the region, he'd never once been consulted about what might be helpful to *him*. Instead, Coast Guard commanders had always simply informed him of what they intended to do and left it to him to make adjustments.

He then began pulling out detailed maritime maps, inviting Sandy to pore over them with him. He pointed out the most dangerous passages he would have to navigate on his next trip and suggested cuts that would make his ship's progress through the heavy ice more direct and safer. He showed her treacherous underwater formations that had taken him years to identify.

Sandy credits the patient, detailed instruction she received on that ore carrier with enabling her to command the *Katmai Bay* effectively in the face of widespread skepticism and with little support. This initial meeting was also instrumental in shaping the leadership style that would serve her throughout her remarkable career.

She says, "I'd been criticized in my earlier assignments for not having an action-hero style of leadership. You know, barking orders, never asking, only telling. The I'm-the-boss-so-don't-you-talk-back approach. I'd also been told that I would never earn respect in this job as a woman if I wasn't willing to always play tough. But what I saw was that asking questions does *not* show weakness—it shows a willingness to learn. It also demonstrates that you have the confidence to listen. Plus it's the very best way I know to build the kind of relationships that strengthen your ability to respond as a leader, and in doing so, to build essential trust."

THE CONFIDENCE TRAP

It's worth noting that both Alan Mulally and Sandy Stosz's confidence was firmly rooted in their competence: in the skills they had acquired, cultivated, demonstrated, and honed over years on the job. This is an important point.

In recent decades, confidence has often become viewed as an almost innate quality, a firm self-belief untethered to actual achievement. Parents who shout "good job!" each time their child takes so much as a step do so in the belief that doing so will boost the child's confidence. Schools that hand out awards to every student regardless of their grades or athletic contributions do so with the same motivation.

The assumption seems to be that positive reinforcement and praise can alone yield confident human beings, but this is a misapprehension. True confidence is always rooted in our sense of our own abilities, along with our capacity—and our willingness—to learn. Confidence ungrounded in actual competence risks exposing us to one of two extremes: a delusional sense of our own greatness, or the imposter syndrome with its fear of exposure.

Since the publication of the influential *The Confidence Code* by Katty Kay and Claire Shipman in 2014, confidence has been viewed as a key differential between male and female success. While the book is highly instructive in showing how confidence can be nurtured, a simplification of the authors' basic idea—that men's confidence is a key reason for their success while women's lack of confidence holds them back—has reinforced the notion that confidence in and of itself provides an advantage to those in the dominant group. The upshot is that confidence has increasingly become viewed as a kind of magic formula that enables those who have it to sail untroubled through life.

As a result, many women have come to view confidence as more of an asset than actual competence, and more essential to building success. Yet because there's no actual *basis* for confidence that is rooted only in self-belief, those seeking to acquire it are often urged to practice positive affirmations as a way to promote self-esteem.

I've encountered this all over the world in training sessions delivered at women's conferences and networking events. It's as if these sessions have taken a page from Stuart Smalley, the *Saturday Night*

Live character immortalized by Al Franken. Stuart, who radiated in-security, would after every humiliating encounter gaze hopefully into his mirror and repeat the immortal lines: *I am good enough, I am smart enough, and doggone it, people like me.* This was particularly hilarious when Franken's character earnestly urged guests who clearly had no need to gin up their confidence to practice affirmations. The classic was Michael Jordan at the height of his basketball career.

These episodes continue to provoke laugh-out-loud moments on YouTube. Yet trainers can still be found urging women and other outsiders to the leadership mainstream to bolster themselves with affirmations—"I am totally confident as I head into this meeting," "I believe in myself on all occasions"—or exchange facile "You go, girl" forms of encouragement. This is all done in the name of bridging the so-called confidence gap with those in the dominant group.

The problem with this approach is not just that it can be shallow and demeaning. It also misrepresents how confidence is actually instilled. Deeply felt and firmly grounded confidence is always the result of demonstrable skills developed through daily discipline and persistent effort. And what we are able to achieve using these hard-won skills.

This is why the notion of someone like Michael Jordan trying to boost his confidence through affirmations is so ludicrous. Not because his dazzling self-assurance makes it feel grotesque (although it does), but because his world-class competence, built up over tens of thousands of practice and playing hours, is what gives his self-belief a solid foundation.

THE PERILS OF OVERCONFIDENCE

As business scholar Tomas Chamorro-Premuzic demonstrates in his wide-ranging comparative research, competence is statistically far more aligned with and predictive of job performance than confidence or self-belief. Yet the value of confidence continues to be consistently overrated. By contrast, competence—often dismissed as "mere competence"—is routinely underrated or disregarded.

This is especially true at the leadership level.

Multiple studies make clear that competence is actually the chief factor in determining a leader's success. Yet organizations often privilege dazzling self-confidence when seeking leaders. As coach Jeffrey Hull observes, "Companies have this huge blind spot when it comes to the kind of individual who presents himself as *the answer*. I say 'himself' because those who take this view are almost always men."

Drawing on a broad range of data, author Chamorro-Premuzic identifies what he posits as the chief reason for this blind spot: a continuing inability among those charged with hiring leaders to recognize *over*confidence as it manifests in men.

He notes that men who exhibit an unwavering faith in their own greatness are often viewed by search firms, boards, and executive committees as masterful and driven: in a word, leaderlike. The result is a disproportionate number of charismatic men who get promoted well beyond their competence level and occupy senior positions for which they are unqualified.

The costs of male overconfidence can be enormous: witness WeWork, Lehman Brothers, Satyam Computers in India, Boeing in recent years. General Motors (GM) spent decades elevating male executives with dazzling faith in their own strategic brilliance in the face of declining profitability. Finally, the board named Mary Barra as CEO. Barra had begun working on the GM assembly line at the age of eighteen in order to pay her college tuition. "Not the strong leader GM needs," was the knock on her appointment. "Competent but boring." Yet her competence managed to stabilize the company.

The Barra example is not surprising, given that Chamorro-Premuzic's research shows that women's confidence almost always aligns with their level of competence (or falls below it) whereas this is not necessarily the case with men at senior levels. Elizabeth Holmes of Theranos would be a high-profile exception.

The reason for this discrepancy is not that men as a whole are so much more confident than women, but that the number of *over-confident* men is far higher. And given that overconfidence and the assertiveness it engenders is often helpful to men in pursuing top positions, overconfident men, though a relatively small percentage of the male population, tend to be overrepresented in precisely those jobs where they can do the most harm.

The inability to spot men with unearned faith in their own abilities penalizes not only women and others in underrepresented groups, but also a lot of highly competent men. Chamorro-Premuzic therefore suggests that it's in the interest of men and women to collaborate on calling out the costs of overconfidence and holding their organizations to account for placing a higher value on competence when considering candidates for top positions.

FILLING THE SHOES

I saw an example of how this can work while on a consulting assignment with a Melbourne-based transport firm.

Ahmet, a top corporate lawyer with an exceptional record overseeing the company's acquisitions, was posted to Singapore to oversee the maritime legal team. The idea was to give Ahmet experience in the field ahead of a potential promotion to CEO. He seemed to have the right profile: he was brilliant, a persuasive speaker with great connections and a dazzling confidence in his ability to lead.

Ahmet was accustomed to people in the company deferring to him, but the team in Singapore was not impressed by his reputation or his brilliance. The problem was that Ahmet knew almost nothing about maritime law, a complex and arcane branch of legal practice, though both Ahmet and the executive team were confident he could quickly get up to speed. Team members in Singapore offered to help with some of the details, but Ahmet assured them he could absorb what he needed without getting into the weeds. "I'm here to set strategic direction, liaise with corporate, keep things on track, and take our reputation to the moon," he said. "The team can handle any technical issues."

Unfortunately, setting strategic direction required understanding technicalities of which Ahmet remained in ignorance. As a result, he quickly began to make decisions based on insufficient information, leaving the team to clean up the mess.

The situation came to a head when the team completed a contract with a shipper flagged in Malta that exposed the company to liabilities they had typically been able to avoid. Ahmet, who'd pushed hard for the deal, blamed the snafu on a few of his team members. They resented it, but said nothing.

But after a second contract created a legal tangle, the corporate leadership team in Melbourne decided to send an ombudsman to Singapore to figure out why the previously competent maritime division was flailing. Melanie, the ombudsman, set up one-on-ones with Ahmet as well as with five senior members of his team, promising confidentiality.

Tracy, an experienced maritime lawyer who was invited to meet with Melanie, says, "I grew up in an Asian culture where you don't question or criticize the boss. It's considered disrespectful and very disloyal. Plus I knew Ahmet was well connected at our headquarters in Melbourne. Since nobody on our team was, being honest about what was happening seemed like a bad approach. But morale was so poor I felt I had to say something for everybody's sake. So I told Melanie that Ahmet was so sure of his own brilliance that he was not open to learning our actual business, which in my view led to costly mistakes, and was earning us a poor reputation."

Melanie heard similar concerns from other team members and took the results of her interviews back to Melbourne. The executive team then made the decision to move Ahmet back to headquarters. He was not demoted, but he was no longer in the running for CEO.

Given the turmoil that the maritime legal team had been through, senior leadership in Melbourne decided to not appoint Ahmet's successor until they got further input from Singapore. So they sent Melanie back to get some suggestions about the kind of leader the team believed could help them be successful.

Tracy says, "It was great when HQ sent Melanie out to solicit our views. HR had been talking about empowering teams but this was the first time we'd seen that in action. Being asked to help in the process gave us the confidence we needed to really speak up, and we all agreed that working for Ahmet for eighteen months had taught us a lot. It had become clear that we needed a leader who really knew how to listen. The problem wasn't that Ahmet didn't know maritime law when he came here. The problem was that he was unwilling to learn. He was so sure of his own brilliance that he saw the details as beneath him. But in maritime contracts, the details matter, so his attitude led to real mistakes. Plus he had no understanding or appreciation for the work the team was doing, so he constantly criticized our performance. This undermined everyone's morale."

Melbourne heeded the team's advice and decided to appoint Ram to head the Singapore team. Ram was a corporate finance lawyer, less senior and less visible than Ahmet, but respected for his collegial approach, the high morale he fostered in his teams, and his eagerness to learn.

The CIO of the company commented, "We got pushback on that decision here at headquarters. Ram's a quiet guy, so some people thought he wasn't 'leadership material.' They seemed to mean that he doesn't present himself as a great leader, whereas Ahmet certainly did. But this episode taught us that being willing to learn on the job is a lot more important than an impressive style or unquestioning self-belief."

LEARNING COMPETENCE

Note that Ahmet had originally been sent to Singapore because his unquestioning confidence in his own abilities persuaded the board to overlook his lack of maritime law experience. Yet it was not this insufficiency that made his appointment problematic, but rather his unwillingness to put in the work required to learn the basics once he had secured the job.

This distinction is important. Confidence is not the problem. Confidence gives us faith that we can develop the skills we need, the tolerance required to learn on the job, and sufficient humility to ask for help and guidance.

*Over*confidence, by contrast, prevents us from accurately assessing the skills we lack and makes us resistant to doing anything about it. Because why should a hotshot like us ever have to sweat the details?

The reality is that almost all of us lack at least some of the skills needed to perform a new job well for the simple reason that we've never done that job before. In most cases, we are only fully qualified for the job we already have. Or for a job we have held in the past.

This simple truth is not always apparent to those outside the dominant group, who often feel they must put extra effort into proving they are absolutely right for a position. They may have been criticized as "not ready for prime time" by those who doubted them in the past, and so fear being judged if they're seen learning on the job. They might be familiar with research showing that those in their group are routinely underassessed on their competence levels. Or they might not have been given sufficient resources and support on previous assignments and want to avoid feeling vulnerable with colleagues they do not yet know.

The upshot is that those from outside the leadership mainstream often feel they need to be ready to perform a job flawlessly *on day one* in order to accept—or even apply—for a new position.

This is quite common. For example, I routinely hear from search firms and HR leaders about women who decline to take the next step in their career because they "don't feel ready," fear they lack the skills, or believe they have "more to learn" in their present jobs. As one headhunter lamented, "I get applications from highly qualified women who *start* by listing all the ways they might not be qualified! Men who have less to offer often convey great confidence, which makes them more likely to get the position. This happens even when a woman is the most qualified candidate, because no employer wants to hire someone who seems to doubt that she can do the job."

WHAT DOES IT TAKE TO QUALIFY?

The impact of this competence/confidence disjunction was on vivid display during a senior marketing retreat I facilitated at one of the world's top medical supply companies. One session focused on the paucity of women who had applied for several new positions the company had posted. A number of women in the room noted that the requirements for the job seemed daunting. They expressed surprise that this had not seemed to discourage some of their male colleagues from applying.

Finally, one woman asked, "When a position lists six qualifications, how many do you need to have? I've always assumed all six would be required but it sounds like some of the guys don't see it that way."

The discussion went back and forth—*do you need five, or would four be okay?*—until Jonas, the chief marketing officer (CMO) for the Americas, stepped forward to share his story.

"I knew ten years ago that I wanted the job I have now," he told the group. "So when a position two levels down came open, I went after it with everything I had. The listing showed five qualifications. I only had two. But I knew that my task was to describe exactly why and how I could pick up the other skills in a reasonable amount of time, which I believed I could do. Nobody expects you to have all the qualifications for the job you're applying for. But they do expect you to have a plan for getting up to speed."

The women in the room practically gasped at his story. The notion that "no one expects you" to have all the skills listed on a job posting was new to them. A few wondered whether the CMO's approach would only work for a man, as they believed women were usually held to a higher standard.

Then one of the women asked Jonas, "How did you *know* that no one would expect you to have all the qualifications listed? You seem to think this is common knowledge, but I had no idea this was how things work. I thought if a posting said five skills, it meant you needed to have those five skills or you needn't bother to apply."

Jonas thought for a moment, then responded. "Actually, it was a mentor I had early in my career who pushed me to apply for a higher position. He told me I had the potential to succeed in that job, and that getting it would boost my career. And he said all I needed to do was convince my potential boss that I was capable of learning what I needed to learn. And willing to put in the effort."

Based on this exchange, the women's network at the company decided to enlist a team of mentors to help female employees get a better sense of how and when to apply for internal postings. This important first step made an immediate difference. When the next list of internal openings was posted six months later, 70 percent more women applied than had done in the posting prior to the marketing meeting.

It's important to note that Jonas, the CMO, did not take the path of overconfidence that Ahmet, the transport company executive, had.

That is, he did not look at the qualifications he lacked and decide "no problem" because he was so brilliant or saw himself as special. Nor did he expect his more qualified second-in-command to assume most of the duties of his job so he'd be spared the task of developing the competencies it required. Instead, he understood and accepted that he would have to work hard to qualify once he had the job.

In other words, he did not view confidence as a substitute for competence. Rather, he recognized that competence evolves, and that our best chance to develop it comes in the course of doing our job.

"LET ME REPHRASE THAT QUESTION"

Even the most confident and successful women, along with those from other nondominant groups, can struggle with feeling unready to move on. Sandy Stosz, the Coast Guard vice admiral we heard from earlier who served as the only female superintendent of a US service academy, recounts a story from the midpoint of her career.

After six straight years of sea duty, Sandy was assigned to the ice-breaker acquisition staff at Coast Guard Headquarters in Washington, DC. Although she hadn't wanted a shore assignment, she found she loved the job. Being the only operations person on a team of engineers and logisticians gave her rich opportunities to learn and to add value. She made a point of telling her assignment officer how grateful she was to have been put in the job.

The day after doing so, he called to ask whether she would like to interview for a position as military aide to the newly installed US secretary of transportation, a cabinet position. (Yes, the same secretary who would later show up when she was installed as ship commander.)

Sandy was surprised that he thought she was ready for such a big step. She explained that she felt honored but, as she'd noted, loved her present job and saw it as a good fit with her skills. She added,

"Plus my team needs me. I don't want to abandon them because I got a better offer."

Her assignment officer was unpersuaded. The next day, he called again. "Let me rephrase my question from yesterday," he said. "*When* will you be available to interview with the secretary?"

Sandy recognized that she was being made an offer she couldn't refuse. So she scheduled the interview, even though she dreaded being evaluated by someone at that level and saw no way she would be selected for the job. Yet the interview went extremely well and she found herself inspired by the new secretary's evident interest in and commitment to the Coast Guard. Nevertheless, she was shocked when she was offered the job, which proved to be the turning point in her career. It broadened her perspective by helping her see where the Coast Guard fit into the bigger picture, gave her high visibility, and provided her with access to the top levels of government and industry.

Two points about this story are important for this chapter.

First, even a woman of Sandy's accomplishments, self-awareness, and grit expressed reluctance at the prospect of a significant promotion because she questioned her qualifications and felt a deep loyalty to the job she had. Second, her willingness to even consent to an interview required a boss who acted like a mentor by rephrasing his request as a clear though subtle order.

By not taking her at word that she wasn't ready, Sandy's assignment officer pushed her into taking an important leap forward.

CHAPTER FIVE

Trigger 4: What Are You Trying to Say?

We rise together by appreciating and learning
from one another's communication styles

No skill is more essential for rising together than being able to communicate our achievements, insights, ideas, and misgivings with clarity and passion. This has always been true, but doing so has become more complex, even loaded, as our organizations and culture have grown more diverse.

People today bring different values, assumptions, concerns, and speaking styles with them to work. This increases the likelihood of our being misinterpreted or misunderstood, and the likelihood that we may misinterpret or misunderstand others. Every time we open our mouth or compose an email or text, we have a fresh opportunity not only to engage and inspire but to baffle or alienate another person. So it should come as no surprise that communications has become our most common everyday trigger.

Yet being aware of the challenge this poses can paralyze our spontaneity and hold us back from showing up as our best selves. Please note that I said our *best* selves—not our most authentic selves. For the truth is that privileging authenticity when it comes to communication can undermine our ability to inform, learn from, and connect with others.

Despite this inherent conflict, we are constantly urged to put authenticity first.

Business media as well as many coaches and experts view authenticity as a competitive edge and a business imperative, not only for brands but for individuals. I rarely deliver a workshop or talk these days without someone asking me how they can claim their achievements, lead a team, or attract mentors while remaining true to their authentic self. Magazines and websites are full of strategies aimed at helping us "shed the mask" so we can be more truly authentic.

It's easy to see the origins of this trend. Those of us who began our careers in relatively conformist workplaces where white men set the tone may have spent decades repressing both our strengths and our vulnerabilities in hopes of fitting in. The same is true for anyone from an underrepresented culture as well as for younger workers, who may resent the pervasiveness of baby boomer values.

Of course, the great value of diversity lies in its ability to bring different perspectives and styles to organizations. The key is balancing what is real and distinctive about ourselves—our perceptions, our values, our cultural background, our homegrown style—with what others find respectful and persuasive. It's therefore usually wiser to focus our efforts on "saying it skillfully," in the words of communications coach Molly Tschang, rather than bluntly speaking our minds in the service of being authentic.

THE AUTHENTICITY TRAP AND COMMUNICATION

I've concluded that the present quest for authenticity should come with a big DANGER sign.

To start with, only our deepest spirit or core distinguishes us throughout our lives; beyond that, we are always changing, evolving, growing. Scientists inform us that every organism in the biosphere comprises trillions of ever-growing and ever-dying cells. To be alive is to be a tiny universe of change.

We know this from experience. Most of us have moments when we look back upon our earlier selves and are appalled by something we said, did, or thought. Yet the very concept of an authentic self suggests that our values, behavior, or speech habits remain unchanging, and that any shift or adaptation is a betrayal of who we really are.

But focusing our energy on being true to what we choose to define as our authentic self can undermine our ability to change and grow. And trying to *communicate* in a way that is effective and persuasive while maintaining our commitment to authenticity can leave us tongue-tied and confused. Most of us learn through trial and error how to convey what we mean by observing how what we say resonates with others. Considering the *they* as well as the *me* is essential.

We can't count on our authentic self—as it exists in this particular moment—to help us do this. And the reputational risks of failing to consider the *they* are multiplying. Every time we log onto Zoom or open our social media accounts, we venture onto contested territory. What we find funny may offend someone whose experience is different than ours. Our chief moral aspiration may be someone else's prime example of political correctness. Our forthrightness in admitting that an assignment has us freaked out may erode the trust of a boss or a team that hasn't worked with us in the past.

In addition, popular mantras—"Let guys be guys," "Speak truth to power," "I gotta be me"—are often used as a license for unleashing our inner jerk. And our most instinctive reactions can lead us to a dead end.

I am reminded of Marshall Goldsmith's experience observing, running, or participating in encounter groups for eight hours a day, month in and month out, while pursuing his PhD in psychology during the 1970s. The goal of these sessions was to relentlessly push participants to share their true, unmediated feelings, to let it all hang out regardless of consequences. But after much digging down and pressuring participants to get ever and ever more real, the true feelings that inevitably surfaced in the group usually fell into one of two categories: either "I hate you!" or "I want to have sex with you!"

Neither response is particularly helpful in the workplace.

I believe we can all benefit by sidestepping concerns about authenticity in favor of working to become more skilled communicators. This requires understanding the essentials that shape how we speak, honing our awareness of what is and what is not effective, and committing ourselves to clarity and professionalism.

ONE BIG ESSENTIAL: RADAR VERSUS LASER

How we communicate is shaped by three components:

- What we notice—what we see and observe, the details that comprise our perceptions
- What we *value* about what we notice—what seems important given how we understand the world
- How we connect the dots in order to tell a story about what we notice—how we convey what we observe and value to other people

Notice is therefore the foundation that informs both what we believe is important and the words we choose to describe it.

This can get tricky because what we notice is shaped by our experience, which can differ depending on gender, age, race, or sexual orientation. People of color may be quick to notice unconscious displays of white privilege. Women are often skilled at scenting out potential male bullies. South Asians in Silicon Valley companies with a high proportion of people from the subcontinent are likely to have a fine-tuned awareness of how caste may shade their boss's perceptions. LGBTQ individuals read homophobic body language with ease.

What we notice serves our survival, as in these examples. But it also shapes how we communicate because it influences the words we choose to describe our perceptions and the stories we tell to connect the dots. It should therefore be no surprise that distinctions in noticing style are a common source of misunderstanding.

A classic and well-documented example occurred when Brooksley Born, one of the nation's top securities lawyers, was appointed head of the US Commodity Futures Trading Commission (CFTC) in 1994. Alarmed to discover a $20–$30 trillion derivatives market that she believed posed a major risk to global economic stability, she proposed stiffening regulations on the least transparent securities held by banks.

But the president's top economic advisers, along with the Federal Reserve chair and the Securities and Exchange Commission (SEC) chief—all men—dismissed her concerns. They contended that the wizards of Wall Street understood their own complex data and that Born was assigning too much weight to external factors. As a result, they advised Congress to block Born's CFTC from regulating the derivatives market. Over the next decade, that market would balloon to $680 trillion and then collapse, setting off the 2008 financial panic, the social consequences of which we still live with today.

Not only Born but a number of other high-profile women, including Federal Deposit Insurance Corporation (FDIC) chair Sheila Bair, "Oracle of Wall Street" analyst Meredith Whitney, and senior female executives at Citibank and Lehman Brothers, spent years in the run-up to 2008 warning about such a scenario. Yet despite their expertise and positional power, these women were relegated to the familiar female role of Cassandra, in the Greek myth, prophesying disasters to no avail.

It's no accident that Cassandra, who foretold catastrophes but was never heeded, was a woman, for female insights are often dismissed as mere women's intuition. The 2008 financial crisis provides perhaps history's most expensive lesson in the differences between how women and men communicate about the world around them.

Born and her fellow Cassandras were unable to get a hearing because, in essence, they *noticed* different things than the men they were trying to warn (the "externalities"). As a result, those they were warning were literally unable to hear how they connected the dots.

Research science suggests a reason, as my coauthor Julie Johnson and I discovered while researching *The Female Vision: Women's Real Power at Work*, in which we explored the role of notice in shaping how we view the world. For example, functional MRIs, which show the brain in operation, reveal that women in general tend to notice a lot of things at once, whereas men in general tend to notice in sequence, one thing at time. As a result, women's attention often operates like radar, scanning the environment and picking up a wide range of clues. By contrast, men's attention is likely to operate more like a laser, focusing narrowly and deeply, and blocking out whatever seems extraneous.

These differences have real-time impact on our decisions about what to say and how to say it.

For example, laser noticers tend to value succinctness, bottom-line data, and the ability to get straight to the point. Because of their focus, they are less likely to be aware of the effect their words have on others, and less eager to qualify their observations or consider scenarios that their data do not account for.

By contrast, radar noticers often like to share plenty of background, including all the details that seem important to the larger story they wish to tell. Radar noticers are also often sensitive to the impact their words are having on others and may include these observations. This sensitivity can make them more open to hearing other points of view.

Given these distinctions, it's not surprising that men may at times dismiss a female speaker as being scattered or beside the point: *Where's she going with this? I can't follow, she's all over the map.* As a result, they may stop listening altogether. Or they may try to summarize what a woman has just said in a meeting so that other men can hear the essential point, which strikes women as pompous and condescending—the famous mansplaining.

Women in turn may view men's laser focus as insensitive and clueless, hopelessly reliant on hard data and resistant to nuance. This may lead them to conclude that men "just don't get it," and to give up even trying to get heard.

The challenge for laser noticers is to recognize the validity of ideas they may perceive as diffuse or randomly presented. The challenge for radar noticers is to discipline their radar so they can communicate in a way that those with more focused notice can hear.

DISCIPLINING RADAR

I got a master class in the need for disciplining radar some years ago when delivering a workshop to the top fifty women in a global biotech firm. Sherry, the highest-ranking woman in operations—cited briefly in Chapter 2—headed the company's huge and lucrative diabetes research and product development practice. At one point, I asked her in front of the group what she believed had been the key factor in her success. Without hesitation she replied, "My ability to be concise."

Sherry explained that, prior to joining the company, she had been a physician in private practice. She said, "I'm from the American South, so I definitely have the gift of gab. But being in practice for twenty years forced me to discipline that and become succinct. As a physician, you often have a lot of complex but vital information to deliver to your patients in a very short time frame, thanks to insurance company restrictions. It's life and death, so you learn to focus on what's most essential. If you go into a lot of detail, you risk over-whelming your patients with too many facts."

This skill served Sherry well in a corporate environment. She says, "In most organizations, there's a kind of male tone that places a high value on being crisp. The senior men I work with tend to have very short attention spans and are only comfortable listening if you *immediately* get to the point. They appreciated that I understood from my first day on the job how to do that. It helped me tremendously, so now I spend a lot of time coaching brilliant women who tend to use a lot of words in their communication to do the same."

Just as women can benefit from disciplining themselves to be more concise and get to the point more quickly, so can men benefit from disciplining themselves to be patient listeners, willing to consider that what they perceive as irrelevant details may in fact be important. And by recognizing that data, grids, and charts do not necessarily tell the whole story.

As leadership guru Tom Peters observes: "Hard—meaning numbers—can be soft; that is, easy to manipulate and useful for confirming biases. And what has long been viewed as soft—building relationships, empathy, intuitive knowing—is very hard. Men can profit when they can admit this."

HONING AWARENESS: WHEN AGE IS NOT JUST A NUMBER

When COVID-19 began to spike across the world in the early months of 2020, most organizations sent people home to work re-motely. As it turns out, this trend has had many unforeseen positive effects. But it further tangled the difficulties posed by differing com-munication styles, particularly across age divides.

For example, a senior executive at a tech company that mostly em-ploys a lot of young millennial and Gen Z workers grew concerned about them when the office switched to virtual almost overnight. "I wanted to know how they were doing and I wanted them to know I cared, so I began a regular practice of calling them by phone. Of course, I rarely got anyone, so mostly I was leaving voicemails. But what surprised me was how few of them called me back. They emailed rather than calling. I decided that the conventional wisdom must be true—younger people tend to avoid actual conversations."

Wrong, says Lindsey Pollak, an author and coach who studies the multigenerational workplace. "The young people she called were probably afraid of interrupting her if they called back. Boomers grew up telephoning people, so they're comfortable with it. But many younger people associate the phone with something going wrong. For them, an unscheduled call from their boss can feel like a precursor to getting fired. Plus they don't use the phone a lot, so may not feel confident about their skills."

Generational differences in communication preferences abound in the workplace. We need to recognize this and take it into account. I often hear baby boomers—my generation—complaining about poor communication skills among younger people, using themselves as a benchmark for how things should be done. A better approach is appreciating the different skills and comfort levels that people of different ages bring. This requires awareness.

Here's Lindsey Pollak's short list of various pitfalls to avoid when communicating across generations:

1. **Consider that words change meaning over time.** Lindsey cites the example of an investment bank that gave junior employees homework. Managers were upset to find that the staffers had, in their view, "cheated" by consulting one another about their answers. The staffers, by contrast, saw themselves as collaborating. Accustomed to doing schoolwork in study groups, they viewed it as simply being productive.

2. **Reframe feedback as coaching.** Keep in mind that junior employees often have little experience being criticized. Millennials may have grown up in small families with relatively older parents who made a practice of encouraging their children rather than offering correction. They may have gone to schools that handed out trophies for participation. So instead of feedback (which, let's face it, few of us appreciate unless we've asked for it), coaching based on our own experience is more likely to be accepted.

3. **Recognize that how you define an acceptable ratio between work and life may not apply.** Ever-faster technologies have increased the pressure on all of us to be available, redefining urgency and pushing work to 24/7. Lindsey's research shows that younger workers are not only less bothered by the work-life balance issues this raises, they often don't recognize a dichotomy, sensibly asking, "Isn't it all my life?" At the same time, having grown up in a world where workaholism is endemic, younger workers are often perfectly at ease pushing back against outsize demands, and comfortable sharing their boundaries: "I'm going to have to leave work at five p.m. this week."

4. **Honor different levels of sensitivity.** Trained since childhood to be aware of racist, sexist, and homophobic remarks, young people often have sharply tuned antennae and push back easily when they feel offended. It's important that those raised differently don't dismiss this as "wokeness," but accept that how we define what's appropriate evolves over time. Effective communicators take this into account.

5. **Keep an open mind about headphones.** This one drives many senior managers crazy. "How can young people who use them possibly be paying attention?" But employees who grew up doing their homework with headphones say that using them helps them be more productive. So it's a good idea to take them at their word, unless you detect a marked dip in productivity.

6. **Learn and respect everyone's name.** Lindsey's exit interviews with younger workers revealed that one of their chief complaints was that the people they worked for never learned how to pronounce their names. "Naming options have exploded in recent decades," she notes, "as names have been become viewed as a means to express individuality. At the same time, organizations have grown more diverse." In this environment, condescension and judgment are disrespectful and demeaning. If an unfamiliar name appears, simply ask how to pronounce it. And then remember.

7. **Ditch the labels.** The media seems to enjoy cramming millions of highly diverse people into categories and giving them labels. For decades, we were subject to constant stories about the imagined "war" between women who work outside the home and women who do not. Since the virtual workplace has made this division mostly obsolete, attention has switched to various alleged wars between people of different generations. This may be helpful if your job is analyzing long-term demographic trends and you're looking for an angle. But in the workplace, labeling undermines our ability to see one another as individuals, blinds us to what others have to contribute, and undermines our ability to communicate in ways that bring us together.

"IT'S OUR ASSUMPTIONS THAT GET US INTO TROUBLE"

Labels are, of course, a form of stereotyping, the habit of making assessments about individuals based on generalized categories. Stereotypes, such as "Young people live online," "Women like to shop" "Men mostly talk about sports," or "Asians work hard but don't speak up," primarily show the limitations of our own experience. And they seriously undermine our efforts to communicate.

Few people I know have more experience helping others to move beyond stereotyping than Bev Wright, an executive coach who had a thirty-eight-year career hiring, developing, and training talent at IBM. Bev is also the current chair of Dallas Dinner Table (DDT), a nonprofit that originated with alumni of Leadership Dallas as a forum for bringing people from different backgrounds and sectors together. DDT originated in response to the brutal murder of an African American man by white supremacists in Jasper, Texas, in 1998.

Bev's first experience at DDT remains vivid because it gave her the opportunity to see her own stereotyping in action. "There was a white man there, a lawyer like me, who was from East Texas. I didn't grow up there, but my parents came from Nacogdoches, and as a child I visited a lot in the summer. And I had a chance to see how grown white men there talked to my father, as if he were not a grown man at all. As a result, I made a lot of assumptions about white men from East Texas. And the first thing I decided was that I did *not* want to sit next to that man. I wanted to sit anywhere else. But of course, that's where I got seated."

Bev's table moderator made clear that the two ground rules of DDT were to "come as you are"—that is, to talk about the experiences that made you who you are—and to listen to others without judging what they said. A tall order in this case, but Bev gave it her best.

"I started by asking the man I was seated with to tell me what had shaped him as a person. And he talked about growing up in a world based on total separation of the races. He said he had not even known until high school that the n-word was not the accepted word. As he talked, he made that world real for me so I tried to do the same, telling him how what happened with my father had made me feel about white men from East Texas. As we spoke, I saw how we'd both started out as blank slates, kids who were imprinted by what we were taught by others. And now here we were all these years later trying to speak about these experiences to one another, being as honest and direct as we could. And it became obvious that the only way we could do that was to move past our assumptions and look at one another as individuals, not representatives of some group."

Bev recalls her first year in DDT as extraordinary because the "come as you are" policy enabled people to share things they usually kept to themselves. "One man talked about resenting affirmative action because he blamed it for killing his father's trucking company. It gave him this grudge, but as he talked it through and we listened without judging, he came to the conclusion on his own that his father had actually been a poor businessman. He realized that he'd been trying to deny that to himself. Speaking about it honestly to people who really listened helped him to recognize this and begin to let his resentment go."

Several of the ground rules at DDT can help all of us move beyond making the kind of generic assumptions that blind us from experiencing one another as individuals, which is essential for communicating with truth and power.

These include:

- Ask questions and then *listen* to the responses.
- Seek to understand rather than reply.
- No debate, no answering back, no contradicting, no "but . . . "
- Remain aware of your own reactions.

"Stereotyping is the lazy person's way to get to know someone," Bev Wright concludes. "It's the opposite of real communication, which requires listening to individuals share their experiences and being willing to share our own. We're often afraid to do this, which is why most diversity conversations lack depth and stay on the surface. But if we don't go deep, we can't build relationships based on trust."

The ability to move beyond stereotyping will only become more important as our workplaces and communities grow more diverse. The writer Jay Kaspian Kang, whose family roots are in Korea, notes the absurdity of categorizing people from twenty countries with wildly diverse cultures as "Asians." He says that "lumping together everyone from Brahmin doctors to Hmong refugees" reveals the absurdity of most demographic classifications, as does the effort to identify this massive group as "white-adjacent."

Like most efforts to assign individuals a group identity, this kind of categorization also inhibits our ability to communicate well. That's because no one—not one of us—wants to be spoken to as a representative of a larger group. We are not typical: we are each one of a kind.

PROFESSIONAL

In the 1980s and '90s, when few women held positions of influence, I was constantly wondering how I could be myself while also demonstrating my potential and finding my place in a workplace culture where confident men set the tone. My self-conscious efforts to adapt often left me either tongue-tied or nervously verbose.

In the following decade, as my work grew more global, I spent a lot of time pondering how to tailor what I offered to meet the needs of wildly different cultures. This added another level to my confusion. Since I was routinely second-guessing my words ("Was *that* appropriate? Should I have said something else in this context?"), I struggled to speak with a clear voice.

Then, my colleague Bill Wiersma sent me an advance copy of his landmark book *The Power of Professionalism*.

Bill makes a persuasive case that thinking of ourselves as professionals can help ground us in a range of situations. For me, this insight served as a lightbulb moment. I realized that much of my self-consciousness was rooted in always thinking of myself as a woman, an American, or both. This focus on identity had the effect of making me feel apart rather than a-part-of.

By contrast, aspiring to be a professional—someone who makes commitments and acts on them in a way consistent with their values but without privileging those values above all else—gave me an instant bond with anyone who had made a similar commitment, regardless of culture or background.

So instead of wondering whether I should be more or less assertive, or whether I needed to calibrate my words to suit those whose experience might be different from mine, I began simply asking myself if a particular response or story marked me as a professional.

When I did, the boundaries I'd been anxiously trying to surmount evaporated.

Professionalism is a great leveler. A young employee can be more professional than a senior manager. A nurse can be more professional than a highly trained surgeon. A hired gun who writes a speech can be more professional than the big shot who delivers it.

Nor is professionalism limited to those in what have been traditionally identified as professional service firms: lawyers, bankers, accountants, and consultants.

Instead, a professional is anyone who adheres to a code of ethics and is diligent and reliable in their work. Bill points out that electricians, hairstylists, child minders, carpenters, and postal and frontline workers can be far more professional than those with advanced degrees. As he says, "Professionals can hold PhDs from top universities or from the school of hard knocks."

Once you start looking, examples of professionalism are everywhere. In Chapter 4, we saw how Alan Mulally assumed leadership of Ford despite having no background as a car guy. What he did bring was a deep commitment to behaving as a professional and holding others to account for doing so as well.

And we saw Vice Admiral Sandy Stosz proving her professionalism by quietly but strategically countering her supervisor's efforts to ensure her failure as the first woman to command a major Coast Guard vessel. Her overconfident, bigoted supervisor was, by contrast, the very definition of unprofessional.

Drawing on Bill's work, here are my own rules for acting and speaking as a professional:

- Professionals respect other people's time—they show up on time and make an effort to speak concisely.
- Professionals exhibit patience—they listen carefully and avoid seeming rushed.
- Professionals don't complain—they understand that things don't always work out as planned, so they accept setbacks and move on.
- Professionals don't engage in gossip—they keep negative observations and stories to themselves.
- Professionals help others to shine—they don't dominate the conversation and are generous with praise.
- Professionals show appreciation—they prioritize thanking anyone who helps them do their job.
- Professionals strive to communicate clearly—they think things through in advance so they can say exactly what they mean.

CLEAR

Let's examine this last point about clarity a bit further. Because being clear is often hard, but essential for effective communication.

In my workshops, I often ask participants to write an intention statement, a quick thirty-second sentence that describes what they most want to contribute in their jobs. This sounds simple but, on the first go-round, I usually get a lot of verbiage, buzzwords accompanied by nonspecific abstractions and generalities: "I seek to be an agent of transformation." "My mission is to unleash our team's full potential." "I am committed to inspiring and attracting the best talent."

The problem with these statements is that they convey no idea of who the speaker is, how they intend to achieve their objective, or why it is important to them.

I ask them to dig down, to get specific. What do you mean by "transformation"? How would you be an agent? What specifically would you do to unleash your team's potential? Potential to do what precisely?

After a certain amount of pushing, participants inevitably break through the verbiage and interrupt themselves: *What I really mean to say is . . . "*

They then offer a clear and concise statement that describes, in personally resonant and compelling language, what they most want to contribute in their jobs.

From a law associate: I want to hold our firm accountable for maintaining its commitment to collegiality by hiring people who treat others well.

From a compliance officer: I seek to train a team that can spot potential compliance issues *before* they arise so we can create a culture of doing the right thing.

From a healthcare manager: I develop written communications that help people understand how our company's services benefit public health.

Leading this exercise always brings home to me how much thought being clear requires—not just when formulating an intention statement, which is inherently difficult, but when preparing to speak about anything that matters. Clarity doesn't just happen. Even the most skilled communicators need to think through exactly what they mean to say, and then find the simplest, most direct words to express their thinking.

When doing this, it helps to engage others. For the fact is, we're more likely to recognize our core idea when we hear ourselves speaking. It's especially helpful to talk with friends or colleagues who will let us know when we sound indecisive or lose our thread. It's no surprise that skilled joke- and storytellers are constantly trying out their material on others.

Clarity also requires using language that our listeners don't need to decipher. So we want to avoid high-flown phrases, buzzwords, and euphemisms. We're more effective when we stick with words we would use when speaking with friends or family members. Also, high-flown phrases encourage us to be overly aspirational, avoiding the nuts and bolts of what we intend to do. Okay, you want to be "a transformation agent." But *how*?

The problem with buzzwords and jargon, such as disruption, customer journey, and growth hacking (let's not even mention humaning), as well as marketing or HR acronyms such as CX, CRM, CRO, and Talent ROI, is that they manage to sound both vague and robotic. Having been wildly overused and applied in a vast number of situations, they've become highly subjective, which means our listeners can never be exactly sure what we mean. As *Inc.* magazine points out, buzzwords and jargon primarily serve to make smart people sound stupid. Fresh language always carries more impact, more punch.

Finally, because euphemisms primarily serve to disguise what we actually want to say, they are by nature imprecise. Yet they increasingly plague our conversations at work and influence how we think of our colleagues. "He's a minority." "She's a diverse hire." What exactly do these statements mean? Is he African American? Is she from Cambodia or the Caribbean? Do the circumstances necessarily require pointing it out? And if they do, why do we shrink from being specific?

It's helpful to recognize that trying to obscure a simple fact under the genteel haze of euphemism inadvertently implies that being direct would be offensive. So while we may imagine we're being "nice" by using a word like *diverse* to describe a human being, we primarily demonstrate that we feel self-consciousness speaking about people we perceive as not-like-us.

Hardly a recipe for rising together.

CHAPTER SIX

Trigger 5: It's Not Fair

We rise together by recognizing the extent to
which "it's not fair" is a losing game

The belief that we've been treated unfairly can trigger us like little else, igniting resentment, anger, frustration, and disappointment. Marshall Goldsmith goes so far as to describe fairness as a "nonstop triggering machine." The machine kicks into high gear because, despite daily evidence that life can be and often is profoundly unfair, we continue to expect that we *should* be treated fairly.

Of course, we should. And in an ideal world, we would. But that's not the world in which most of us live and work. The real issue is how we handle ourselves when we perceive that we've been treated unfairly. Do we address the situation directly and try to defuse it? Or do we blow up any perception of unfairness into a full-scale grievance? And how do we work with those we believe have benefited unjustly?

These are explosive questions, especially when gender, race, or ethnicity get thrown into the mix. One key to assessing how to address them is to determine their relative degree of importance. This can be tough to do in the post-MeToo era, when we've been encouraged to be vigilant about sensing harm. In particular, many younger people entering the workforce have been primed by their university experience to be on the lookout for microaggressions and microinequities, sometimes equating them with active discrimination, harassment, or racism.

Certainly, egregious or persistent patterns of bias require the enlistment of HR, and potentially the legal system. Systemic issues need to be met with a systemic response. But what about the less grievous situations that routinely crop up and have the power to wound us, keep us stuck, and derail our relationships? What about our everyday perceptions of unfairness?

Being prepared to address these on an individual basis is essential if we are to rise together. It does no good to simply suppress our feelings, fuming inwardly while attempting to move forward. This can make us feel diminished and we may end up disengaging from a job we otherwise enjoy. But taking the opposite tack—making a public point or filing a formal complaint—can and often does backfire. We therefore want to think carefully about bringing out the big guns because we didn't get the promotion we expected or we object to our boss's leadership style.

HUMBLE PIE

Erica, a talented leader in a global financial company, confronted the fairness trigger early in her career. She and her colleague Louis were selected to colead an innovation incubator that their bank was setting up to explore new ways to reach small business.

Erica says, "I was the creative type, good at innovation, plus I'd had experience with small business customers. So I saw myself as a perfect fit for the incubator. I knew Louis because we'd been hired into the company at the same time and done our training together. I liked him but saw him as an in-the-box thinker, a by-the-book corporate type. I was surprised when the higher-ups chose him for the project, but figured they probably wanted someone more invested in the status quo to balance the creative energy on the team."

The incubator enjoyed quick success and several of Erica's ideas for customer partnerships were put into action. Then the bank decided to make the laboratory a full-fledged division of customer marketing. "I assumed I'd be chosen to head it," says Erica. "I had the experience and the skill set, plus the team looked to me for solutions. So I was stunned when Louis got the promotion, even though, in a way, it was not surprising since the bank was very good at promoting men."

Erica tried to swallow her disappointment, but having Louis as her boss was a struggle from day one. "I could not get over my resentment at working for someone I viewed as less qualified than I was. I knew Louis could sense this, so I kept waiting for him to say something, even though I knew he was conflict-averse and it was pointless to expect it. Needless to say, our relationship grew strained, which affected the whole team. We got our work done, but inside I was seething."

Things came to a head one afternoon when Louis vetoed a project that Erica had been developing with a group of retail customers. "I felt humiliated at the prospect of telling those retailers that an idea I'd persuaded them to sign onto was a no-go, basically letting them know that I had very little power. I was furious, and decided I should probably go home early. I figured if I stuck around, I'd end up telling Louis off."

As she was heading out of the office, she heard Louis raving about a new bakery that had opened near their office. Thinking to console herself with some outrageous treat, Erica stopped by on her way home. She had decided to buy a delicious-looking cream pie when the expression "humble pie" suddenly came into her mind.

"I don't know where the phrase came from, but suddenly I realized that what I needed to do was eat some humble pie. That is, I needed to accept that I was not chosen for the job. It may have been unfair,

and it probably was. But it wasn't helping *me* to be a martyr in my
own mind. And it was ruining my relationship with Louis, who after
all was now my boss."

Erica bought the cream pie. And when she got home, she pulled
out her watercolors and made an elaborate label to stick on the box.
Amid flourishes and curlicues, it proclaimed:

THIS IS HUMBLE PIE FROM ERICA

The next morning, she walked into Louis's cubicle and set the box
on his desk. He stared at it for a moment, then said, "You? *Humble?*"

That cracked Erica up, and they both started laughing. She says,
"We kept laughing until our sides ached. Then Louis opened the box
and cut two huge slices and we sat there in his cubicle, stuffing ourselves. People were staring. They weren't used to seeing us together.
And besides, who eats cream pie after breakfast?"

When they'd finished eating, Louis looked Erica in the eye and
said, "I have a feeling there's something you want to tell me."

With her anger defused by the situation, Erica was able to be honest. "I told him I found it hard to report to him because I believed
I should have been given his job. I said I thought my skills were a
better match and that I'd contributed more to the incubator. Plus I
believed it was unfair that the bank always seemed to promote men,
even when women were qualified."

Louis told her he'd been aware of her resentment but kept hoping it would pass, which he admitted wasn't the most courageous
approach. Then he pointed out that this was no longer an incubator project, it was a *management* project, which was different. "To
get promoted into management, there are a lot of boxes you have to
check," he said. "That's what I was busy doing while you were being
creative. So if your goal is a management position, maybe we should
talk about what you can do to make that happen."

As Louis laid out what he believed was required, Erica realized
she had no interest in checking the boxes in the way he had done. "It

finally registered on me that the company had chosen him *because* he's very status quo and diplomatic, someone who fit right in with the management culture. That's not who I am or who I want to be. I told him that, and he said, 'Fine. So let's talk about what path could work for you.'"

That kicked off an ongoing conversation that helped Erica clarify the kind of career she actually wanted. "Louis had suggestions about how I could better position myself. It was really helpful because his perspective was so different from mine. Suddenly, instead of a rival, I had this well-placed ally who was helping me see the bigger picture, beyond this one job and this one promotion."

Looking back, Erica believes that her truly out-of-the-box move with the pie broke the tension that had been eroding her ability to work with Louis. It signaled her desire to get honest about her resentment, but in a way that showed generosity and a sense of humor. She says, "Taking this kind of wacky action got me out of my victim frame of mind. I was the one who had been carrying the resentment, so I was the one who needed to address it. The pie was an impulsive gesture, but it proved to be the turning point. Not just in that job, but in my career."

GRIEVANCE AND CULTURE CHANGE

Erica believed, and still believes, that gender played a role in her not being promoted. But she made the decision not to focus on it. "I recognized that if I did, it would give me a reason to hang onto my grievance by making it a social issue. It was more helpful for me to view it as a signal to start thinking more seriously about where I wanted to go."

A decade later, Erica found herself in a senior role in which she was often called upon to counsel women who believed they'd received unfair treatment. She says, "Their perception that gender played a role was usually not off the mark. Unfairness *exists*, it is very real, even though things are slowly getting better, at least in our company. But if it's not threatening or outrageous, I think it usually pays to find a way to defuse it. That doesn't mean repressing your resentment. That never works and it can eat you alive from inside. But it does mean finding a way to take action so you can move forward without burning your bridges."

Erica's approach raises an important question. Don't we risk undermining our organization's ability to make progress if we treat examples of everyday unfairness as personal roadblocks to be managed and overcome rather than as opportunities to challenge the larger system? Isn't breaking some eggs necessary if we aspire to be a positive force for long-term change?

This truism is true as far as it goes, but it ignores the reality that the person doing the breaking often gets broken along with the eggs.

The reality is that power politics always play a role in how decisions are made in organizations. So we don't want to take the system on naively. As leadership guru Peter Drucker never tired of saying, "Decisions are made by the person who has the power to make the decision." Not necessarily by the best person or the wisest person or the most qualified or insightful, but the person who has the power by virtue of position.

When we challenge that decision-making in a public way, we are taking on the power structure. So unless we have an extremely compelling issue *and* strong support from well-positioned allies, we may find ourselves just hanging out there as people we hoped, or assumed, would back us make themselves scarce. This sounds harsh, and it does not reflect how most of us would like the world to operate. But where power lies must be taken into account if we choose to challenge the system.

In addition, addressing routine inequities on an individual basis does *not* mean abandoning the push for larger change. Given that companies generally become more fair, just, and equitable as a consequence of their leadership becoming more diverse, whatever increases the likelihood of those who have experienced unfairness rising to positions of authority and influence has the potential to spur systemic change. So working to become as successful as we can may in fact be our most effective route to building a more fair culture.

THE QUEST FOR A LEVEL PLAYING FIELD

Letting go of our *it's-not-fair* radar can be tough for many reasons. One is the strong emotional response most of us have when we perceive that we've been treated unjustly. Another is the social and political environment, which over the last decade has encouraged a focus on grievance and division and kept us on high alert for any potential harm. Terms such as *microaggression* make this clear, as do accusations of "reverse privilege."

But we also struggle to align our expectations with reality because we are primed to believe that our organizations operate—or should operate—as meritocracies, rigorously allocating rewards in proportion to contribution. The underlying premise of meritocracy is that those who work hard will be rewarded, which by extension implies that anyone who loses out must somehow have failed.

Although most of us know from experience that being in the right place at the right time and connecting with the right people (often through sheer coincidence) has played a pivotal role in shaping our path, we often prefer to attribute our success entirely to our own efforts. We can be reluctant to acknowledge the role played by fortune, good or bad, because doing so might make our lives and careers feel random and diminish the pride we take in our own efforts.

Extremely successful people in systems that claim to be meritocratic often justify massively outsized rewards by citing how incredibly hard they've worked—as if a single parent holding down two or three jobs in order to make ends meet might enjoy similar blessings if he or she would only buckle down. In this way, people tie themselves into mental knots and assume indefensible positions rather than admit one of the world's most obvious truths: that luck, circumstances, and the conditions of birth and parentage disproportionately advantage some people and disadvantage others. And that, while hard work is usually a factor in success, it is rarely on its own sufficient.

The language of sports, widely used to describe our lives at work, can also mislead our expectations in regard to fairness. Sports teach many useful lessons about persistence, grit, teamwork, and the patience required to develop complex skills. But the culture of sports offers little help in environments where policies must constantly adjust to shifting business conditions, technological disruptions, global reverses, and evolving leadership commitments. Although we often speak of it as such, a career is not a game. The conditions that shape organizations are never static and ground rules vary in response, so the game analogy rarely applies.

Nor does the metaphor of the "level playing field," which is also adapted from sports, translate into how most organizations function.

Sports exist in the physical world, which means that good design and the right equipment *can* make the actual field or surface of play sufficiently level to avoid anomalies that consistently favor one side or the other (the Monster Wall at Fenway may be an exception). In organizations, by contrast, the field is metaphorical, an imagined ground on which individuals with wildly differing advantages start at different levels and encounter different hurdles. Getting the lay of the land may require inside information. A curve ball means one thing on the mound, another in the performance review process. The ground in organizations is always shifting beneath our feet.

RULES? WHOSE RULES?

Or take the notion of rules. Here too, sports analogies can be misleading.

Sports take place in a defined space and time and follow rules that can be listed, referred to, adjudicated, and appealed. This makes it possible to decide what is objectively fair within those bounded parameters. In addition, in sports the umpire or ref always has the final say. Even the person on the field with the most actual power—the manager, the greatest-of-all-time superstar, the owner—can get tossed if he or she mounts a too-strenuous objection.

In sports, rules triumph over position.

Organizations, by contrast, operate according to stated but also un-stated rules and reflect diffuse or opaque lines of authority. To take a flagrant example, the strategic plan for the entire company may have been devised by an outside consultant with zero investment in its execution, which means there is no one to appeal to when things go wrong. Influence and personal relationships also play an outsize role in determining where power is vested in organizations, which is one reason that rules-based objections often get ignored. In organizations, power and rules dance around one another. Of course, this is also true in a sports franchise's front office, as opposed to on the field of play.

Questions of fairness, potentially fluid in organizations, can create an environment in which we are quick to contest one another's beliefs because our differing experiences shape wildly different interpretations. This keeps the culture in turmoil in way that can have both positive and negative effects.

On the positive side, people from nondominant groups have over the last few decades been relentless in raising awareness about the role bias can play in hiring, promotion, and assessing performance. As a consequence, those in decision-making positions are now far more likely to recognize and seek to address systemic unfairness. For example:

- *Why are there no women on this list of candidates for the VP spot?*
- *Could these criteria disadvantage minority candidates?*
- *Should we cast a wider net instead of always favoring graduates of elite schools?*

Such questions, common today, were rarely raised in the past. As Marshall Goldsmith observes, "There has probably never been a time in history when senior leaders were less racist and sexist than they are now. But there has also never been a time when more complaints are being lodged."

While these complaints do keep the pressure on the larger culture, adopting a negative focus as individuals can keep us stuck, setting us against one another, deepening divides, and igniting our human tendency to pass judgment. Resentment may cause us to restrict workplace socializing to people we perceive as being like us, or seeking confirmation for narratives about how *we* never get a fair shake because . . . (fill in the dots). Or we may turn inward, losing heart and concluding "it's just not worth it" because we feel unappreciated and disregarded.

In this way, the fairness trigger can undermine our capacity to make the best of our talents, collaborate broadly, focus on the big picture, and enjoy our work. The negative energy that drives many *it's not fair* narratives can also diminish our ability to effectively advocate for the larger changes we seek to see put in place.

WHEN WE GET CAUGHT IN THE CROSSFIRE

As companies seek to create more inclusive cultures, those in the dominant group (white men in much of the West, Japanese men in Japan, etc.) may find themselves in the grip of *it's not fair*. The toxicity this creates can get out of hand when a leadership shift upends settled expectations.

A few years ago, I worked with Alex, a young designer in a large automotive parts manufacturing firm. As the only male in his industrial design school study group, he had entered the workplace believing he had better relationships with women than with men. But that belief was tested when his company unrolled a high-profile effort to hire, promote, and develop more women.

The initiative began after a well-publicized study by a global consulting firm ranked Alex's company in the bottom fifth of its sector in regard to female representation above the admin level. Shortly after this finding made headlines, the CEO called a news conference to announce the company's commitment to quadrupling its female representation within the next five years, doubling promotion rates, and becoming an "employer of choice" for women.

"We plan to move fast," he declared. "It's a brand-new day. Watch us."

A new HR team was hired away from a competitor and tasked with reviewing the company's criteria for hiring and performance. They uncovered significant examples of unfairness.

- An automated recruitment software program penalized anyone who had taken a career break, which disproportionately affected women.
- Salary was often adjusted to reflect what the candidate had previously earned, which meant low earners continued to earn less.
- Performance reviews for white men routinely referred to their "potential," an assessment that rarely appeared in reviews for women or people of color.

Based on this information, the HR team developed new benchmarks and put the company's leaders through a two-day training session. In addition to addressing specific inequities, the team also adjusted managers' pay to reflect the number of female employees they promoted over the year. Outcomes were graded on a curve, which ensured that managers would compete against one another.

Alex, immersed in the details of headlight design, paid little attention, though he was aware that several women who had been hired when he was were now quickly moving up. He says, "I tend to avoid office politics and believe our leaders are generally fair, so I figured the women who got promotions must have earned them. Some of the guys were grumbling, but I knew to steer clear of that."

The situation became more challenging for Alex when his manager sent him to an unconscious bias intensive delivered by an outside diversity consultant that the new HR team had brought in. "It was an offsite and I had a travel delay, so I arrived at my hotel late at night after the orientation," Alex recalls. "When I got to my room, I found a box on the bed labeled 'Check Your Privilege.'"

Accompanying the box was an envelope containing blank slips of paper and instructions. Participants were supposed to write down every privilege they had ever enjoyed. Alex says, "My family was fairly poor but my parents managed not to get divorced, so I put down intact family. I'm smart, but I wasn't sure if this qualified as a privilege. I had to work my way through design school, which meant it took me six years to graduate, so I didn't consider my degree to be a privilege. Of course, I knew enough to write down *white male*, though being male doesn't seem much of an advantage in the company right now, unless you're already at the senior management level. But I figured if I didn't put it down, I'd get called out in one of the sessions."

His intuition proved correct. The next morning, the trainer read everyone's statements aloud, voice checking every white male as privileged. The trainer then asked the participants to talk about how writing what they had made them feel, being as honest as they could. "Don't be afraid to really let loose," he urged. "You're in a safe space here."

A number of the women, especially those who had been with the company for a while, said the exercise had made them realize what a raw deal they'd been getting. Alex recalls, "They gave examples of all the times they'd been dumped on by men in the company. And all the times their contributions had been overlooked or they'd been targets of degrading comments. Some of the stories were terrible and you could see why a lot of the women thought men were clueless and entitled. A few women even brought up their experiences with online dating. The trainer kept encouraging them to dig down and share more details."

Hearing so many negative stories about men, Alex struggled not to feel defensive. "I kept wanting to say that I was different from the guys they were describing, and point out how I hadn't gotten a lot of breaks. I also couldn't help thinking how the company was now *paying* executives to promote women and wondering why that didn't qualify as privilege. But I knew that if I said any of this, I'd be seen as a bad guy. The whole thing felt unfair because the women could say whatever was on their minds but I knew I couldn't. It felt like a setup."

The next week, Alex's manager called him in for a debrief. Alex made a few comments about the format but said nothing about how irritating he'd found the session. "I didn't want my manager to lump me in with the guys here who are always complaining about women. I'm not like them. I don't see it as a bad thing if women are getting some breaks now because men got a lot of those breaks in the past. What I *don't* like is being assumed to have privilege I don't believe I've had, and having my experience discounted. Plus, knowing I can't be honest about how this feels for me."

Alex had been triggered by perceived unfairness but he dealt with it in a constructive way.

- He acknowledged, at least to himself, what he felt.
- He didn't blame the individual women he worked with for the shift in the playing field.

- He didn't complain that the goal posts had moved, another sports-based metaphor with limited relevance for the world of work.

Instead, Alex recognized that his company's leadership was attempting to shift its culture because they believed it was the smart thing to do. He accepted this and he got on with his work.

However, to make this approach sustainable, Alex will need to be able to air his experience and share his observations with colleagues and potential allies. So far, his company has not provided a way for this to happen. Instead, the new HR team has ignored the impact their new policies are having on men, especially those who are early in their careers. Having his experience discounted may over time spur Alex to disengage.

FROM THE BOTTOM UP

Watching how Alex's company tried to institute brand-new-day change reminded me of a contrasting approach I wrote about decades ago in my book *The Web of Inclusion*. I was profiling the *Miami Herald*, which had historically been viewed by a large number of its employees as a divisive and deeply unfair culture. In addition to the antagonistic divide between the business and editorial sides that one typically finds at newspapers, those who worked on the English and Spanish editions rarely communicated. A physical wall had even been erected between them because the English speakers found the Spanish-speaking employees "too loud." The wall was routinely cited as a metaphor for the larger culture.

In order to shake things up, the *Herald* hired a new publisher, Dave Lawrence, a newspaper executive with a reputation for bringing people together and instilling an ethic of excellence. Under his leadership, the paper would go on to win five Pulitzer Prizes.

Near the start of his tenure, Dave announced a "fairness initia-tive" aimed at identifying what the *Herald* needed to do to become a fairer place. But rather than bringing in consultants or charging HR with devising and implementing new policies, Dave took a bottom-up approach, recruiting a team of forty employees to form a fairness task force.

Team members were drawn from every level and division, with a fairly equal representation of senior and junior people, of men and women, and of English and non-English speakers. The purpose of the task force was to identify where people throughout the company perceived unfairness and to come up with recommendations based on that. The only ground rule was that the entire group had to reach consensus on every suggestion they endorsed.

Team members set up suggestion boxes around the company and asked people to write down experiences and stories about what-ever felt unfair, retaining anonymity if they chose. They then read through every piece of paper. Team members often disagreed on the validity of what was reported, but because they had to reach consen-sus, nothing was dismissed. This made for very long and often heated meetings.

As one participant told me, "The process ended up taking six very long months. It really tried my patience because reaching consen-sus with people who have different experiences and opinions is time consuming and painful. But what I learned was that getting on the same page with someone requires you to listen to a lot of things you may disagree with, not judging but trying to understand the other person's point of view. Doing this over and over changed me as a human being. And what I learned is that you can't change an orga-nization unless the *people* in the organization change. Asking people with different experiences to work together until they find agreement is probably the hardest way to do anything, but that's why in the long run it's effective. Also, because so many people are included in the process, you don't have to work afterward to get buy-in, which saves you time and trouble in the long run."

When at last the task force presented twenty-six recommendations, Dave Lawrence's leadership team signed off on every one. Dave then asked task force members to work with HR to identify specific policies and practices that could make their suggestions a reality. Again, this was not a rapid process, because a lot of people were involved and because working groups were asked to come to consensus on what they decided. Task force members virtually had to train HR in the collaborative process they used; some in HR were resistant and one senior leader left. But the relationships that developed as the group worked through volatile issues resulted in widespread trust that this was the right approach.

The long-term impact of the fairness task force was extraordinary, with staff members later attributing the paper's ability to support the community and keep publishing during a catastrophic hurricane as the direct result of how they had learned to work together. "We could never have done it before," said the paper's managing editor. "We were too focused on internal battles, on protecting what we saw as our turf. Plus, we didn't have relationships outside our silos. It's only because we learned to work with people we thought we had little in common with that we were capable of a really heroic effort."

Decades later, I still view Dave Lawrence's approach as the most effective route for addressing issues of fairness. Giving everyone a forum to share perceived inequities and having the process managed by employees at a range of levels who work to achieve consensus is always going to take longer and be messier than handing the task off to a team of professionals. And focusing on fairness for all rather than fairness for one group, regardless of how much that group has struggled with unfairness, is always going to win broader support.

The *Herald*, like Alex's company, used literal boxes as part of its change initiative, but those boxes sent a very different message.

- "Check your privilege" asked people to identify all the ways they might be different from one another, and to categorize their experience using assigned language, even if doing so didn't feel true for them.
- "Share your experience" asked people to identify what felt true for them without labeling it. This increased the likelihood they would be able to hear one another and perceive what they had in common. This approach gave everyone involved a chance to be heard and feel valued, a precondition for building a culture of fairness.

Retired brigadier general Tom Kolditz, former chair of the Department of Leadership and Behavioral Sciences at West Point, offers another lesson in addressing fairness. Tom's distinctive twist on the put-yourself-in-someone-else's-shoes metaphor enabled him to create opportunities for people in his department to share one another's experience, and to learn from doing so.

Tom had noticed a number of men on his staff griping about privileges they believed were accorded to women. "I wish *I* could leave at four o'clock every day to pick up my kids," was a common complaint. Tom says, "So I told them, 'Just start doing it. If you need to pick up your kids, pick them up. I'm not asking anyone to punch a clock here. Just do what you need to do and get your work done.'"

Once the men began taking him at his word, they found that taking short breaks to address personal commitments was not at all disruptive. They stopped complaining about the women getting special privileges. Says Tom, "Plus there was an unexpected bonus. As the men stepped up and to take care of more personal tasks, they began managing their time a lot more efficiently—as the women had been doing all along!"

CHAPTER SEVEN

Trigger 6: The Grapevine and the Network

We rise together by knowing how to develop,
extend, and leverage our networks

The fairness trigger has the power to push us into silos of identity-based complaint, an understandable but unproductive response, and one that can set us up for a whole new cascade of triggers. I routinely hear from women who assert that women have made "virtually no progress" in the last twenty or thirty years, an assertion that anyone who's been around for a while can easily dispute. I also hear from men who claim they have scant chance of promotion in a world in which "women and minorities get all the breaks."

Such beliefs are tough to maintain in the real world—that is, the world outside narrative-reinforcing bubbles. These bubbles develop when we spend too much time in single gender or racial-, ethnic-, or sexual preference–based groups in which trading unhappy stories serves as a way to bond.

Of course, we all need to let off steam from time to time, and inequities continue to exist and can be very painful. The problem arises when commiserating becomes a habit or a way to confirm our sense of belonging rather than a spur to constructive action.

When commiseration rules, our networks begin to operate like grapevines. It's an important distinction. Let me explain.

Since the American Civil War, the term *grapevine* has been used to denote an informal system for sharing and amplifying information, facts, warnings, stories, and gossip.

Grapevines flourish in systems where official, usually top-down, information is either closely held or widely mistrusted. As a result, grapevines are most likely to operate among those who lack power, for whom they can serve as a vital source of information that may, or may not, be accurate. Of course, grapevines also flourish notoriously on social media, where they enable misinformation and rumor to go viral and circle the globe.

Grapevines can gain a foothold in established organizations, institutions, and communities. They are most likely to form when a weak or self-interested leader withholds information, creating a vacuum that needs to be filled, even if only by rumor and complaint. Grapevines also take strong root in cultures in which whole groups of people feel excluded, disempowered, and disaffected. As such, pervasive and active grapevines are classic markers of dysfunction.

Grapevines can create echo chambers among people with similar experiences because they provide a way for us to confirm our assumptions, beliefs, and biases without having to test them against contrary facts or opinions. Echo chambers often favor and accentuate negative stories whose sensational nature makes them tempting to share. As a result of this algorithmic peculiarity, grapevines tend to amplify grievance and can instill a cynical or pessimistic mind-set among those who receive and pass along information.

Being privy to information shared through a grapevine can make us feel as if we're *in the know*: an insider, a pivotal link in a vital chain, a powerful node in an essential web. Yet grapevines do little to augment our actual power. They're about talk, not action. They do not lift us up, though they can give us an effective tool for dragging others down. As leadership coach and master network facilitator Bill Carrier eloquently notes, "Grapevines bear no useful fruit. Only a bitter wine that can be addictive."

Addictive is an accurate description. Grapevine behaviors such as gossiping, trading stories, and bonding over grievance can become a habit, a default we revert to because those around us routinely indulge. We may feel pressured to participate because doing so provides us with a way for us to fit in. Or we may believe that listening to other people's grievances gives proof of our empathy.

But we need to think carefully about how well this serves us.

A client of mine, Daniela, had an epic struggle with an unsympathetic supervisor that she resolved after a great deal of angst. Afterward the head of her division offered a helpful piece of advice. "You handled a bad situation very well," she said. "But you brought way too many people along on the journey. I know people here talk a lot, but you have too much potential to waste your time feeding the gossip mill."

THE HEALTHY NETWORK

The opposite of a grapevine is a healthy network, one that operates on the principle that what's good for one is good for all. Because of this positive orientation, healthy networks encourage mutuality and reciprocity, providing us with multiple points of leverage that enable us to broaden our connections and build our skills, even as we help others to do so as well.

Healthy networks reject backbiting and chronic complaint. Instead, we talk up fellow members, who talk us up in turn. We recommend, advocate for, and take actions that help one another to advance. We share resources, connections, ideas, and solutions. By embedding us in a web of alliances and diverse relationships that build upon one another, healthy networks augment our power in the world and help us rise together.

Bill Carrier notes that, in every network, people assume one of three roles: contributor, neutral, or threat.

- Contributors are always on the lookout for opportunities for others, actively making recommendations, providing contacts, and sharing resources.
- Neutrals are part of the network because people either like them or want to associate with their status. Neutrals *may* prove helpful to others, but they aren't proactive about it and may be unavailable when others approach them.
- Threats view the network instrumentally, as a tool for self-gain, seeing contribution through the lens of quid pro quo. Because threats feel little loyalty to the group, they may also feel free to gossip and trade inside information, weakening solidarity and trust in the network as a whole.

Having worked with networks for decades, Bill has found that healthy ones protect themselves by discouraging the kind of venting and negativity that grapevines tend to thrive on. He says, "No network is entirely free of back-channel conversations, but they cannot be allowed to diminish the group as a whole. Backbiting and telling tales are corrosive, so strong networks will not tolerate those who demonstrate these behaviors for long. Over time, habitual self-seekers will get frozen out."

Bill also notes that, to maintain itself, a healthy network must find a way to deal with venting and complaining, practices that drag us down rather than lift us up. By encouraging a negative mind-set, habitual complaints also make it more difficult to get things done.

Bill says, "The purpose of a network is to provide tangible support that helps people reach the goals they set for themselves. Venting beyond a certain point drags everyone down, so a good network will find a way to block it."

FROM OBN TO ERG

Old boys' networks (OBNs) have long served as vehicles for helping men to rise, smoothing their path by providing mentors, visibility, information, and support. OBNs have also traditionally served organizations as an organic way to identify, vet, and advance potential leaders, while defining and defending key aspects of the culture. In this way, OBNs provide members with a strong sense of belonging, as well as a serious leg up. Although their insularity and impenetrability hardly qualify them as healthy networks, they have historically been superbly functional for those who operate inside them.

Their downside has always been their exclusivity. They're great if you qualify as an old boy—typically a man with a specific background, education, and set of connections or memberships, sometimes going back generations. But if you don't fit the profile—if you're a woman, Black, or part of any nondominant or recently arrived group—you've historically been out of luck.

OBNs used to dominate organizations, defining who mattered and who did not and determining who had access to key resources. In some companies, they still play this role. But as organizations become more diverse, OBNs have increasingly become viewed as problematic because they draw from such a narrow talent base. High-functioning organizations over the last few decades have tried to address this by casting a wider net as they seek to identify future leaders and give them the resources and connections they need to move ahead.

As a result, a range of alternative networks have sprung up and spread inside organizations. They may be informal or grassroots webs, founded by people seeking strength in numbers who also want to smooth the path for others like them. Or they can be formal networks, usually organized and run by an executive champion or a unit within HR. These formal networks tend to have clearly articulated goals and objectives, such as addressing the attrition of women and minorities or branding the organization as inclusive.

Both informal and formal networks can be highly effective, though it's worth noting that the best formal networks usually assume an informal character, reflecting the personalities and interests of the people who are most active within them as well as the web of relationships they bring.

Employee resource groups (ERGs) are a prime example of formal networks that help expand access and resources for those who may have been isolated or excluded in the past. The first ERG was founded in 1970, when Xerox initiated a Black Employees Caucus in response to continuing discrimination in the company despite the CEO's personal commitment to fairness. The goal was to create points of access and connection for employees who had been underrecognized and underserved, giving them a stronger voice and more career support.

Diversity pioneers such as AT&T and IBM followed suit and expanded the trend to include networks for women, LGBTQ employees, and a range of ethnic minorities. Over the last two decades, organizations large and small have set up these networks, often first in the US but increasingly across the world. My work has given me a front-row seat from which to witness their development.

I've seen these networks evolve from well-intentioned but often marginal gatherings with tiny budgets and little structure into real power centers that provide tangible benefits to those who join and attract senior leaders to serve as sponsors. I've observed them become integral to how organizations deliver leadership development and training. And I've watched these groups lose their grapevine orientation.

For example, in the early 1990s, I worked with a lot of beta-stage women's networks. Whether formal or informal, their primary purpose often seemed to be giving women a safe place to talk. Given their lack of structure, these networks often defaulted to shared laments about unfairness or generic affirmations of the "You go, girl!" variety.

While having a venue in which to air complaints did instill a sense of belonging among participants, it often exacerbated feelings of powerlessness. In addition, support in these early networks was often defined as simply listening, empathizing, and offering emotional backing, rather than taking specific actions to help one another move ahead.

This shifted as these internal groups began adapting some of the practices of traditional OBNs, putting the focus on mutual advancement but losing the elitist bias. Establishing mentoring circles, matching members with sponsors, sharing connections, and focusing on leadership skills helped transform many ERGs into healthy and highly effective networks. Their positive impact has been amplified as those who've benefited from participation have moved into senior positions fired with determination to "pay it forward" to those coming up.

Of course, internal networks are not always powerhouses. In some cases, they may be too formal because of their officially sanctioned nature, whereas classic OBNs were always highly informal. Formality and structure can limit the role of personal chemistry, which is key to successful mentoring and sponsorship. Or these internal groups may remain stuck in defining support as listening and sympathizing rather than as providing advocacy and shared connections.

When this happens, external networks can fill the void.

GOING OUTSIDE

A superb example is the Olori Sisterhood, a highly effective network of Black female political operatives in New York. These women— fundraisers, lobbyists, staffers, and public relations specialists—are passionate about politics but prefer to exercise behind-the-scenes influence rather than running for office themselves.

The Sisterhood dates back to 2009, when a group of Black male political operatives, many of them close colleagues of the women, organized a strategy meeting in the state legislature from which women were pointedly excluded. In response, a group of women decided to hold their own meeting, which the men promptly tried to crash. That broke up their meeting, but the women decided to continue getting together, in coffee shops or one another's homes.

At the time, many of the women felt both unseen and stuck. Despite working like demons and being showered with praise for their efforts, their advice was often ignored and they struggled for influence. Most of the promotions in their field went to men whose well-established OBNs—white, Black, Latino, or mixed—gave them a strong advantage in the tight-knit world of political advisers. While the women had connections, they seemed unable to leverage them in a way that gave them a real boost.

From the start, the Sisterhood served as both grapevine and network in that the women spent time sharing professional horror stories and helping one another emotionally through various life crises, including challenging pregnancies, painful divorces, and the complexities of caring for aged parents. But their commitment from the start was to build their individual and collective power. To that end, they adopted OBN practices.

For example:

- When one of them got an audience with a high-profile political player or was interviewed by a media outlet, she talked up her sisters' skills.
- When one of them secured a new job, she fought to hire other Olori members.

- When one of them secured a valuable contact, she shared it with the group instead of jealously guarding it.
- When one of them had a high-stakes meeting coming up, the group convened a strategy session to help her.

Through it all, they relentlessly hammered on the message that their network was not just about them and their careers. It was about becoming a resource for helping Black women claim a seat at the table and become recognized as an unstoppable political force.

After more than a decade of fierce mutual advocacy and shared mutual gains, the women moved from local campaign work to heading important lobbying firms and serving as sought-after political consultants for national candidates, which enabled them to have impact on a bigger stage. When they spoke, aspiring candidates listened. When they faced criticism, someone spoke up on their behalf.

And their male colleagues stopped excluding them from meetings.

MUTUAL ADVANTAGE

The Olori sisters built their own healthy network. But joining one that's already established can also boost our careers while giving us the opportunity to be of benefit to others. Eddie Turner, a motivational speaker, executive coach, and consultant with the global HR company Linkage, is a good example.

Eddie began his career in IT, joining a major corporation in Chicago back when the internet was new and anyone who understood how it worked was viewed as offbeat but necessary. He says, "In the early days, employers weren't looking for an IT degree, they were looking for a certificate, which I quickly got. I had real skills and worked hard to outperform my peers, because my parents had drilled it into me that, as a Black person, I had to be the best if I wanted to have a chance. It wasn't long before I was running the CEO's meetings and everyone was telling me how valuable I was."

Eddie, however, was filled not only with a desire for excellence, but a desire to lead. "That came from knowing how many people behind me had no opportunities. I believed that if I could aspire to leadership, I should try. So I began pushing for a job that would put me on a leadership track. But I kept getting the same response: that while I had the skills and experience, nothing was going to happen unless I got a degree."

Eddie applied to several Chicago-area colleges, basing his potential choices on convenience and affordability. "When I told my boss what I was doing, he gave me some of the best advice of my life. He said, 'You go to school to get an education, but you also go to build a network. That's just as important. You're in Chicago, which means you want to go to Northwestern.'"

Eddie did so. And when he got his degree, he resumed pushing for a job that would position him for leadership. To his surprise, he continued to get turned down. "Before, I was always told that I had the experience but not the degree. Now that I had the degree, I was told I didn't have the experience. It felt very unfair and was hard to process emotionally. But the response I got made it clear that I needed to find another employer if I wanted to rise and test out my full potential."

Eddie decided that the best way to get started was to attend the regular networking events that Northwestern offered its graduates. He not only attended, he got active—offering to run them, handling the IT, suggesting topics, and recruiting fellow graduates. He became, in Bill Carrier's definition, a contributor.

His efforts drew the attention of a participant in the group. "After one of our meetings, a man named Bob Dean came up and offered to be my mentor. As it turned out, he was a senior VP at the search firm Heidrick & Struggles, so he knew a whole lot of people. He told me, 'My gray hair will open doors for you.' And that's what happened.

He had access to powerful people and he introduced me, vouched for me, and became my advocate. He helped me develop the connections I needed to stand on my own."

Although Eddie's Northwestern degree didn't get him the promotion he'd expected, it ultimately gave him something more important: the network he needed to position himself as a potential leader. It also gave him a networking orientation that transformed his understanding of how to effectively pursue his goals.

Eddie says, "That experience taught me that your connections are your most important asset and a key part of how people see you in the world. So I've continued to build and expand them no matter what else I am doing. Right now, I'm a member of the National Speakers Association, the American Society for Training & Development, the International Coaching Federation, and the 100 Coaches Network."

As with his Northwestern alumni group, Eddie doesn't simply join. "I look at how I can play an active role. I volunteer to lead meetings. I identify people I want to know better and follow up with them one-on-one. I make a point of asking how I can help them. So now I have this big, rich, diverse, and ever-expanding network that helps me *and* all the people I'm connected with. Social media has only made this network more powerful. And it's made it much easier to keep in touch."

Eddie prizes his healthy networks because of their positive focus. "I avoid conversations where people find common ground by complaining or talk about how powerless they feel," he says, describing the typical grapevine orientation. "I think it's counterproductive because it undermines your motivation. And in my experience strong motivation goes hand in hand with a commitment to excellence. Staying positive is essential."

Eddie notes that whenever he feels tempted to gripe about the unfairness of a situation, he thinks of someone like Jackie Robinson.

"I know I've never gone through anything like he and the people in his time did, so their stories fortify me. They had so much grit. And they made it possible for someone like me to be where I am. Also, you can't see the impact of your path when you're on it, so you never know when your enthusiasm might help someone else. That's why getting active in a network is so important. By banding together, you make life better for everyone."

STAR POWER

Eddie recognized that he had no possibility of breaking into the OBN at his original employer, no matter how hard he worked. Going outside the company to build his connections turned his career around. This is by far the most productive approach whenever we find ourselves being excluded. But there are other advantages to doing so as well.

For example, building our external networks can help us make better career decisions and understand our own strengths. That's because participating in a network broadens our perspective—not just about what might be available, but about our present situation. This was an unexpected conclusion in Harvard Business School professor Boris Groysberg's extraordinary study of the relationship between individual talent and organizational culture, *Chasing Stars*.

Groysberg wanted to test the widely held belief that individual talent is the prime determinant of success in knowledge-based enterprises. He did so by running an eight-year, in-depth study of Wall Street analysts, a classic example of top-tier knowledge workers. The study made clear that, like many knowledge stars, these analysts routinely overestimated their own value. They also *under*estimated the role their organizations played in providing a platform that supported their own performance. As a result of this misplaced emphasis, these high performers assumed that their skills were more portable than they actually were. In fact, Groysberg found that the performance of the majority of star analysts declined sharply when they left the firms in which they had flourished.

Analyzing his extensive data, Groysberg was surprised to find an exception. The performance of female analysts was actually more likely to improve than to decline after they had made a move. Because his quantitative study could not account for this anomaly, Groysberg began interviewing female analysts in order to discover why this might be true.

He found several reasons.

First, the female analysts tended to have much stronger external networks than the men, typically because they'd been excluded from the OBNs inside their firms. These networks provided essential support as they transitioned to their new positions, whereas the men's OBNs were no longer available to them once they'd left their companies.

Second, the nature of the women's experience—in particular, having seen brilliant female colleagues fall by the wayside because they'd been undervalued—made them more skeptical of the idea that individual brilliance alone is sufficient to account for star performance. This made them far more diligent about analyzing any potential move in terms of whether it provided a good cultural fit.

Finally, the women tended to draw on their networks to help them decide whether they should make the move: whether the new job was a good fit for their skills, whether the company was the kind of place they would enjoy working, and whether their new position would enable them to build lives that were sustainable and rewarding.

By contrast, the men in Groysberg's study were most likely to base their decision to move to another firm solely on salary and bonus. Unfortunately for them, viewing increased compensation as a "no-brainer" often ended up undermining their value in the analyst marketplace. Because they failed to recognize the resources showered upon them in the cultures that had made them successful, they ignored the extent to which their former firms had enabled them to flourish.

Among these star analysts, then, access to internal OBNs often proved to be a *disadvantage*, at least among those who ended up taking their talents elsewhere. More useful were external networks that adopted the practices of OBNs.

NETWORK TACTICS

Spending time in echo chambers and grapevines can trigger us into thoughtlessly dismissing those we perceive as "not like us." Does this mean we should avoid participating in networks of people who share our experience? Not in the least. Such groups can be a rich source of support, enhancing our confidence, deepening our sense of connectedness, expanding our resources, and strengthening our resilience. They can also teach us network behaviors, giving us practice in the mutual exchange of both tactical and strategic support. The Olori Sisterhood provides a great example.

The problem arises when these groups inhibit rather than sustain our ability to build strong relationships with people *outside* the circle. By consorting primarily with those we perceive as similar to ourselves, we narrow our frame of reference. By defaulting to our comfort zone, we make it harder to connect across boundaries of gender, culture, race, and hierarchical status. And we may lose our tolerance for risk.

My late friend and colleague, the diversity pioneer Roosevelt Thomas, talked about the key role that referent groups play in helping us map our place in the world. He observed that those outside the power structure are often most comfortable in such groups, which he defined simply as clusters of people who share our experience and with whom we identify.

Roosevelt noted that sticking only to our referent groups can affect our behavior in ways that undermine us and diminish our capacity to grow.

For example, we may come to feel uncomfortable with gossip or negativity in the group, but fear seeming disloyal if we try to shift the conversation onto a positive track. So we end up making cynical comments in an effort to fit in. Or we may lose our chops for connecting with those we view as different, becoming awkward, self-conscious, and unsure of what to say because our referent group makes it easy to default to our comfort zone.

To avoid this trap, it's helpful to ask ourselves whether our referent group is operating as a grapevine or as a network. If our participation triggers emotions that reinforce our sense of separation from those outside the group, we are probably caught up in a grapevine. If our participation triggers emotions that make us feel connected to the wider world by giving us secure ground on which to stand and from which to move forward, we can be confident that our referent group is serving as a healthy network.

STANDING OUR GROUND

Grapevines thrive on defining who's in and who's out. The stories and information we share are the currency we trade, the proof and measure of our value. In networks, our value lies in our ability to build relationships that benefit others as well as ourselves. But to do this effectively, we need to believe we have something to offer. This is why healthy networks require confidence while also helping us to build it.

But what if we don't *feel* all that confident? What if we believe others in the network have more to offer than we do? What if we're not sure that we really belong?

Such fears are common, especially when we suddenly find ourselves in a network that expands our potential to connect across a range of boundaries, or asks us to broaden our understanding of who we are and what we have to contribute. There are various ways to address this trigger of insecurity. For example, we may want to enlist one particular ally to help us get started. But I'd like to share a simple method that proved startlingly effective for me.

In 1995, Marshall Goldsmith invited me to join The Learning Network (TLN), a small group of authors, speakers, and consultants in the field of leadership. Because most of us worked alone and spent a lot of time on the road, we didn't have the chance to meet many colleagues. So Marshall figured it would be helpful to bring a group of us together to serve as colleagues for one another and provide a core network of support.

I loved the idea. I worked with aspiring women leaders around the globe, work I found deeply satisfying but also rather lonely. I often envied the women in my client companies, who worked together on a daily basis, whereas I was always flying in and out. I had wonderful, inspiring experiences and responses, but then was off to my next engagement. I had a lot of friends but knew virtually no one who did what I did or shared my highly independent way of life.

Eager to participate, I showed up regularly at our TLN gatherings. Yet I struggled to believe that I really belonged. The problem was that I felt intimidated by many of the members, most of whom were men, many of them superstars with huge reputations. Well-known, eagerly sought after, and spectacularly rewarded, these men commanded center stage at major conferences where I delivered small breakouts. At the time, women's leadership was far from a hot topic, so I struggled for visibility and was not particularly well paid. Now, suddenly cast in with a lot of big shots, I felt like an also-ran.

Marshall kept saying that the purpose of our group was "to help one another and make all our lives better." This implied some degree of mutuality, the bedrock principle of a network. But while I certainly saw how *I* might benefit from most of the people in TLN, I believed

I had little to offer these mostly wildly successful men. As a result, I spent most of my time bonding with the handful of other women. Without knowing it, I was turning what was intended as a robust and high-powered network into yet another single-gender referent group.

One evening, Marshall threw a party for us at his house outside San Diego. As usual, I was seated with a couple of the women, enjoying their company and sticking to my comfort zone. At one point, I noticed four of the men I found most intimidating enjoying a boisterous conversation. They looked like they were having great fun and I found myself wishing they'd ask me to join them—waiting for one of them to make the first move, as if this were a high school dance.

Then one of the women in my group began talking about how much my work meant to her because my focus on women's strengths and contributions had given her more confidence in herself. Suddenly, I realized the extent to which I was selling not only myself, but the work I believed in, short. By indulging my own insecurities and clinging to a picture of myself as less-than, I was diminishing the value of what I contributed to the world.

It was time to take a risk.

I rose, walked across the room, and stood with the four men I'd been passively wishing would invite me to join them. I didn't say anything; they were engrossed in their back-and-forth. I just *stood* there. I decided that this was all that was required of me at the moment. Standing up with the big guys was enough.

They didn't particularly acknowledge me, but they didn't seem irritated or affronted. They were just men doing their thing, having a good time. I maintained my position. I did not decide that not being instantly included in their conversation meant they found me unworthy. I did not slink off. I tried to send the message through my physical presence that I belonged, that I was one of them.

At last, one of them asked me a question and we began to talk. Others joined in and the conversation grew animated. I felt an intense sense of accomplishment: I'd gone from circling the edges to positioning myself in the center of the network. I was ready to be part of the larger whole.

In that moment, the network became my referent group, expanding my notion of who qualified as being "like me." By letting go of self-consciousness, by tolerating the discomfort that risk inevitably stirs, I was able to stand in solidarity with those I had perceived as other. Securing this broader ground through my own efforts enabled me to imagine how I might contribute to the group, and how I might ask for help.

In time, I grew skilled at both.

CHAPTER EIGHT

Trigger 7: That's Not Funny!

We rise together by getting humor right

Early in my career, I worked as a speechwriter for perhaps a dozen senior executives, all of them men. I soon lost count of the number of times I got a midnight phone call in my hotel room at some conference from a frantic boss scheduled to present the next day. "Can you find me a few good golf jokes by tomorrow morning?"

Pre-internet, this was a tough assignment at that hour. I soon began traveling with lists of jokes.

At the time, I wondered where it was written that male executives always had to begin a speech, or even preface brief remarks, with a joke. Those I wrote for seemed to take it as an article of faith that starting off with a few witticisms, no matter how obviously canned, hastily told, or beside the point, would establish them as having a personality and therefore earn them the right to proceed to be as dull as they liked. At this most of them were masters, packing their presentations with masses of data projected onto a screen at which they would often stare, sometimes even turning their backs on their audience.

Their listeners would roll their eyes and wait for it to be over. But they would nevertheless do the speaker the courtesy of laughing at their jokes. This of course irritated me to no end, since the speaker inevitably interpreted it as proof that his technique was working. Which meant he would insist on kicking off his next talk with more prepackaged jokes.

People, especially women, would come up to me afterward to commiserate. "I suppose *you* had to dig up those jokes for him?" Or they'd lament, "Well, that was torture. Does he think we haven't heard that story about the frog in boiling water?" Or simply, "Someone needs to let him know he can't tell a joke!"

My unspoken response was always, "Why don't *you*?"

Of course, no one ever did. When the person telling a joke holds a position of power, people will usually yuk it up, which assures that we'll all continue to be treated to shopworn efforts at hilarity. This constitutes a minor annoyance in the scheme of things, but the compulsion a lot of men have historically felt to try to be funny—and, once they believe they've succeeded, quickly pivot back to business— is emblematic of how humor can serve as a trigger in the workplace.

HUMOR AS TRIGGER

Life has evolved since my speechwriter days, when executive was shorthand for male and assistants were sometimes advertised for in newspaper classifieds as "gal Fridays." As the workplace has grown more egalitarian, comments that were once routine (*"Honey, can you type this up for me?"*) have come to seem sexist and out of line. In the process, humor has grown complicated. A thoughtless attempt at levity can turn a room stone cold. An ill-judged witticism can blow up a meeting, or a reputation.

Navigating potential humor triggers in such a sensitized environment requires skill and intentionality. We need to consider the potential nuances of what we propose to say, and understand how our quips might be perceived by those with a different background and experience. Unfortunately, this level of calculation can be tough to reconcile with the insouciance and spontaneity that humor at its best relies on.

Back in the day when men, usually from similar cultural backgrounds, dominated the workplace, humor played a less controversial role. Men often reaped outsize rewards for being viewed as funny. "He's a great guy, you'll love him, a real stitch" was a common endorsement. Having a good repertoire of jokes (as opposed to relying a speechwriter to dig them up) was the easiest way to get known for a sense of humor. Jokes also provided the routine currency of relationship, signaling comfort with the culture. "Have you heard the one about . . . ?" served as a way to bond.

By contrast, today many jokes have become problematic, serving as flashpoints or a way to distinguish who understands that the culture and the rules are changing and who does not: "I can't believe he would tell that joke. Did he bother to look at who was in the room? Clearly, he just doesn't get it."

This awkward state of affairs can leave some men yearning for a past when humor was humor and you didn't have to scrutinize every witticism. This in turn can extend to the charge that the newcomers to the workplace—women and ethnic or racial minorities—are humorless. Or the belief that humor has now been effectively banned from work.

NO JOKING MATTER

As we consider the triggering impact of humor, it's helpful to differentiate between humor and jokes. Jokes typically suffer from a twofold problem.

First, jokes are by nature transgressive. That is, they are funny precisely because they juxtapose or conflate two opposing interpretations in a fresh and often outrageous way. They are good to the degree they are surprising, so they rely on a degree of shock. It's no coincidence that former or would-be comedians who took to talk radio to spout their views became known as shock jocks. Or that many of them made their names by directing their fire at what they saw as uppity women.

As shock jocks know all too well, jokes routinely mine stereotypes, often those of race and gender, upending or exaggerating them for effect. This is why so many jokes are offensive—some mildly, others profoundly—and deemed unfit for "mixed company." Since company is now definitely mixed—at work, in politics, in the whole public realm—a big proportion of jokes are now off the table for anyone seeking to maintain a professional reputation.

Jokes are tough because deliberate misunderstanding rooted in stereotyping and unexpected juxtaposition provide their snap. This is true even for my old speechwriting bête noire, golf jokes.

Harry returns home after 18 holes with his buddies.
His wife asks, "How'd it go today?"
"It was great until the third hole. Then, Charlie had a heart attack."
"Oh, no! Poor Charlie. That's terrible!"
"It was. The next fifteen holes were all, hit the ball, drag Charlie. Hit the ball, drag Charlie. A real pain."

This classic relies on conflating two wildly different interpretations of what constitutes terrible. The humor lies in how it confounds expectations. The stereotyping is minimal and benign (empathic wife, golf-obsessed husband). But mild and patently silly as it is, it's no longer a joke that anyone would use to kick off a meeting.

It's not really offensive, but it's not appropriate either. Someone in the room might be suffering from a heart condition. Someone's husband might have had a heart attack last week. So it's no joking matter. Plus, the cultural context—husbands golf, wives wait at home for them—can be viewed as condescending, or simply be lost on employees whose experience lies in a different realm.

The upshot of the need to be sensitive is that would-be humorists are left to search for jokes that are actually funny but which could never, under any circumstances, offend anyone.

Good luck with that.

In addition to relying on stereotype and juxtaposition, jokes can feel subtly aggressive because they virtually announce, *"Now, I'm being funny."* This creates the expectation, even the demand, that others will laugh, regardless of whether or not they think it's amusing. As noted, if the person telling the joke holds a position of power, everyone will probably titter away, however stiffly. But if a power differential is not at play, the listener may decline to allow the aspiring humorist to define what qualifies as funny.

The joke teller may then experience this refusal to go along as rejection, especially if he (or she) places a lot of stock in being considered funny.

Baffled, he may give it another shot.

"You don't like that one? How about this?"

No laughter.

"How about *this*?"

Still no laughter.

"You all need to lighten up."

Tip: If we hear ourselves telling others that they lack a sense of humor or need to lighten up, we probably need to rethink our approach to humor. Quite simply, this is no way to bond. Or to provoke a laugh.

Similarly, if we hear ourselves telling a third party, "I'm sorry if I offended her. Too bad she can't take a joke," we need to accept the possibility that *our* definition of funny is the problem. Our efforts to raise a laugh are probably perceived as manipulative, or out of sync with the audience or the situation. This puts us at odds with the lively and engaging spirit of good humor.

THE HERITAGE OF WORKPLACE HUMOR

Until fairly recently, things were not so constrained. When men with similar lives were bunched around a conference table, there seemed little need to ponder whether someone might frown on this or that witticism. Everyone in the room was acclimated to just going along, so no one was looking to take offense.

Let's be clear. It's not just men who risk going astray when stepping into the role of would-be entertainer. I've watched women fall on their face with ill-timed quips and barbs that depict men as clueless, self-regarding, unable to listen, or too dense to make intuitive connections. Attempting to bring the spirit of Sarah Silverman into the conference room rarely works.

Attempts at generational humor aimed at Gen Z, X, Y, or the always-good-for-a-chuckle boomers also routinely fall flat, displaying questionable taste and arousing resentments. As noted in Chapter 6, no one appreciates being typecast or categorized; it affronts our individuality. So while flippant generalizations on the subject of age may provide red meat for stand-up comics—whose *job* is being provocative—they can read as galling in the workplace, sowing division and supporting a culture of us versus them.

Of course, endlessly trying to assess what's acceptable and what's not can be exhausting. The upshot is that some very funny people find it easier just not to go there.

"I've cut way back on my quips in speaking," says Tom Peters, who's been addressing audiences around the world since the publication of his iconic bestseller *In Search of Excellence* in 1982, and has always been known for his sense of humor. "I feel like I'm becoming a lot duller these days, but there are too many ways being funny can give offense. There's a lot of edginess out there, a willingness to judge on a perception or a word. It can be a minefield, so it's better to avoid it."

RETROFITTING HUMOR

All this may seem to indicate that humor in the workplace is becoming a threatened species. To the extent that this is true, we need to mount a rescue mission. At its best, humor can break the tension in a room, deepen bonds between teammates, charm an audience, close a deal, or simply make the daily experience of work more enjoyable. Humor also enables us to exhibit spontaneity and let off steam, especially in stressful environments. It gives us a way to demonstrate confidence and warmth.

For all these reasons, humor is far too valuable to be banished.

Rising together depends on getting humor right. Precisely because humor can serve as a potent means for uniting as well as dividing, we can all profit from using humor to bring people together. The question is how to proceed.

I've been grappling with the issue for decades, first as a speechwriter, then as an author, professional speaker, and leadership coach. I have watched talented executives fail at funny, discussed fine points with master speakers, and interviewed coaches who help clients use humor more effectively. What follows are some thoughts about how to undertake the essential task of retrofitting humor for a different kind of workplace.

SELF- AND SITUATIONAL AWARENESS

Getting humor right in a sensitive environment requires that we be both self- and situationally aware.

Being self-aware requires understanding *why* we want to tell a particular story at a particular time. Is it solely to be funny? Or are we also trying to make a point? Perhaps we're looking to score points with someone in the room. Maybe we're trying to cloak a resentment or put someone in his or her place with what seems to us a subtle dig. Or we're genuinely attempting to defuse a tense situation.

Whatever our motivation, simply taking a minute to ask, *What is my purpose in saying this?* can help us avoid many humor pitfalls.

Situational awareness is also key. This requires asking ourselves whether this is the time and place for the humorous observation we have in mind. And considering as well how an observation that strikes us as amusing might resonate with people whose life experience and upbringing is different.

Recently, I worked with an energy company in Houston that was trying to integrate women and people of color into what had been a very traditional engineering culture, almost entirely male and white. The CEO—I'll call him Richard—was a great guy, warm, and very well liked by people at every level. He'd recently shown that he was serious about making his company a better place by the way he'd handled a sales leader who was in the habit of denigrating female engineers.

Richard told him he needed to change his tone, but the man pushed back. "I'm your top producer, which tells me I don't need to change my style," he said. "I am who I am, and I call 'em like I see 'em."

Richard sacked him on the spot.

I usually met with Richard in a conference room. But one morning, he invited me into his office. As I took a seat in front of his massive desk, I noticed a small sign facing me—and every other visitor. In big block letters, it read: BE BRIEF, BE BRILLIANT, OR BE GONE.

The message did not square with the man I'd been working with. So I picked up the sign and turned it in his direction. "What's the story with this?" I asked.

Richard looked at it blankly. "Oh, I forgot it was even there. Someone gave it to me as a joke. I thought it was funny."

I said, "I know our purpose in working together is to build a more inclusive culture in your company. I'm wondering how this sign supports that aim."

Richard shrugged. "No one has ever complained."

"Well," I said, "since you're the boss, it's unlikely they would. But that sign is pretty intimidating. I mean, expecting *everyone* who walks through your door to be brilliant? And essentially telling them to take a hike if they're not?"

I handed him the sign, and he tossed it in the wastebasket.

"I guess I wasn't thinking," he said.

He was right. In this instance, Richard had lacked situational awareness.

INTRINSIC HUMOR

Situational awareness is also key to using intrinsic humor, humor that relies on details that strike us as ridiculous in the moment, rather than relying on jokes or preplanned witticisms. This is a particularly helpful path forward for women, since research tends to show that women who employ zingy one-liners often get tagged as snarky. Instead, noticing incongruities in a situation and highlighting them in a way that provokes surprise can be highly effective, bringing people together while also lightening the tone.

Intrinsic or situational wit can be quite subtle, conveyed in a gesture as well as a word. Madeleine Albright, the first woman to serve as US secretary of state, demonstrated this with great aplomb. Two years into her service as America's top diplomat, the FBI arrested a Russian intelligence agent sitting on a bench outside the State Department monitoring a high-security meeting room outside her office via a listening device. It was the first known breach of the building in history.

Secretary Albright summoned the Russian foreign minister to meet with her the following morning. She needed to let him know that the breach had been discovered and would not be tolerated. She thought long and hard about what she should say, but in the end settled on an indirect but highly effective approach.

Secretary Albright was known for her huge collection of pins, which she deployed on jacket lapels and dresses, usually to identify an allegiance, mark a holiday, or provide implicit commentary on a meeting. For this occasion, she dug down into her capacious jewelry box and selected a truly enormous and unmistakable bug crafted of gold, onyx, amethyst, and tiny diamonds.

When she walked into the room where her Russian counterpart was waiting, she looked at him, and then glanced down at her jacket with pointed directness. The pin clearly conveyed her message: "We know exactly what you've been up to."

When she looked back up, the stone-faced minister was chuckling. He nodded to signal that he'd gotten the point. They were then able to hold a productive discussion. And the Russian embassy abandoned its efforts to spy on the secretary's office—at least during Albright's administration.

COMPARTMENTALIZED HUMOR

Intrinsic or situational humor relies on awareness. It does not broadcast its intention, but draws from the circumstances at hand. This stands in contrast to the more compartmentalized or deliberate forms of humor that have traditionally been deployed in organizations.

Compartmentalized humor is used intentionally, usually at the start or conclusion of remarks, though it may also be inserted in hopes of providing a comedic break. The point is that it's inserted, rather than surfacing as with intrinsic humor, which means it usually requires a frame. Frames such as "Did you hear the one about . . . "

or "A funny thing happened to me on the way here . . . " send a clear signal: *Now I am going to be funny.*

Compartmentalized humor, when it fails, seems both generic and beside the point ("Why's he wasting our time with this?"). Intrinsic humor, when it fails, tends to confuse ("I'm not sure I get the reference"). Compartmentalized humor serves primarily as a means of showcasing the storyteller's skills (or trying to). Intrinsic humor creates a bond based on the serendipity of what compels notice.

Given these differences, it's not surprising that men, who have traditionally been rewarded when they use compartmentalized humor with skill, tend to rate themselves highly for *initiating* humor. By contrast, women tend to award themselves higher marks for *appreciating* humor. Intrinsic humor must be surfaced to be appreciated.

Of course, identifying women as preferring intrinsic humor and men as using compartmentalized humor is a stereotype. Not all women use intrinsic wit and not all men compartmentalize their attempts at being funny. Also, we evolve over time. Two decades ago it was widely accepted in the comedic world that "women can't succeed at stand-up." Women might be hilarious playing characters on stage or screen, where humor derives from context. But in comedy clubs, men held the stage and took the heckling. This has now changed, fed in recent years by female phenoms who use platforms like TikTok and Instagram to test run their routines and build their followings.

Understanding the differences between intrinsic and compartmentalized humor can help us all become more adept at using comedy to our advantage. Men serious about connecting with women can benefit by recognizing that women may view jokes less as clever icebreakers than as tools for distancing or peacocking: *Look at me; don't you think I'm funny?* Women can benefit by taming the irritation stirred by men seeking to elicit what feels like unearned laughter.

THE HUMOR OF VULNERABILITY

Intrinsic humor is more likely to provoke the laughter of recognition ("That's me too!") than the laughter of admiration ("That guy's a hoot!"). For this reason, intrinsic humor is more likely to be self-deprecating, comfortable displaying vulnerability.

A wonderful example was shared by Naomi Bagdonas and Jennifer Aaker, coauthors of *Humor, Seriously*, based on a course they teach at Stanford Graduate School of Business.

A CEO was delivering the first virtual meeting with his executive team a few days after the initial COVID-19 lockdown. People were exhausted and frightened, so the situation was tense. The CEO talked through the situation, shared a few slides, then turned the meeting over to a colleague while leaving his screenshare on. Everyone assumed he had simply forgotten to turn it off. But what then appeared on everyone's screens was their boss opening up Google and typing into the search bar, "things inspirational leaders say during hard times."

Everyone laughed. The CEO had succeeded magnificently not only in making fun of his own insecurity in an unprecedented situation, but addressing a reality that nobody was quite sure how to respond to. And like Madeleine Albright, he did so without having to say a word.

Self-deprecating humor can be extraordinarily effective because it demonstrates vulnerability (as with the CEO: "See, *I* don't know what I'm supposed to do now either"). At the same time, self-deprecation also serves as a powerful if subtle means of demonstrating that you are self-confident enough to let your vulnerability show.

But self-deprecating humor comes with a caveat.

It's most effective when you are in a position of relative power. The more authority you have, the easier it is to stir up a laugh by poking fun at yourself. This is why examples of self-deprecation shown by especially powerful people stick with us for decades, becoming legend.

Returning from a state department trip to France where his wife dazzled everyone with her charm, President Kennedy famously opened his next press conference by saying, "Allow me to introduce myself. I am the man who accompanied Jacqueline Kennedy to Paris."

After a year of being fiercely criticized for his laissez-faire management style, Ronald Reagan stepped to the podium during the Washington correspondents' gala and genially observed, "It's true that hard work never killed anybody. But I always figure, why take a chance?"

Self-deprecation at this level betrays supreme confidence. It sends a message: *Hey, I'm comfortable being human*. But it can be trickier if you're in a junior position or one of the few women in the room. In these situations, self-deprecation can come off as a lack of self-confidence, or an effort to draw attention to your own powerlessness.

For example, I recall being in a large meeting to which a junior female employee had for some reason chosen to wear flip-flops. When called upon to speak, she tripped twice on her way up to the podium, not an uncommon occurrence when wearing these flimsy shoes. As she took center stage, she giggled, "Someday, I'll get it together!"

The sotto voce response: "Let us only hope."

HUMOR GONE AWRY

Of course, the responsibility for rescuing humor doesn't fall only upon would-be humorists. How we respond to the efforts of others to lighten the mood or inject levity plays an important role. But this can get sticky. In today's sensitized environment, it can be hard to distinguish genuine efforts to amuse that nevertheless go awry from the employment of wit in the service of hostility. And even when we make a distinction, we may not be sure what to *do*.

We can start by establishing a clear bright line about what is never acceptable. Racial, ethnic, and homophobic jokes; attempts at mimicry and accents; or making fun of peoples' names do not belong in the workplace, *ever*. Nor does sexual innuendo or the kind of routine harassment that tries to excuse itself as jesting.

But painting bright lines that exclude these practices is not just a job for HR. Team leaders also need to set some bounds. This is usually best done in a positive context.

For example, at the start of a project: "Being able to laugh together is going to get us through good days and bad over the next few months. That's why we can benefit from a few guidelines. Here are three simple things that are not going to work. Does anyone have any other suggestions?"

As individuals, we also need to let people know when we feel they've crossed a line. If it's clearly egregious—say, a racist joke—we'll need to respond on the spot, and be as direct as we can. For example, "I found what you just said unacceptable and demeaning, as well as unfunny. Please don't talk that way in my presence." This kind of firm response will help you and those around you process what just happened. And, unless the would-be jokester is totally dug in, it should help him clean up his act.

Yet it's also important to recognize when humor is simply clueless or hapless, because the potential for overcorrection is always present. Treating a humor misfire as a hanging offense creates tension, undermines collegiality, and can be unfair. As Tom Peters observes, "When we're constantly on the lookout for anything that might give offense, we tend to retreat, and so do the people around us. This undermines the spirit of freedom that engagement, creativity, and collaboration depend on."

It's usually a good practice to address cluelessness, but we can do so most deftly if we assume the other person acted with positive intent. The CEO with the BE BRIEF, BE BRILLIANT sign planted on his desk was demonstrably a person of goodwill, so simply pointing out how others might perceive the sign was the right tactic. Good people and good leaders usually want to know whether their attempts at humor might send an unintended message.

Saying it skillfully, as Molly Tschang advises, requires a softer approach. Molly notes that plunging in immediately with a forthright, "That wasn't funny!" or "I find what you said offensive" serves as a declaration that can foreclose discussion. As a result, such responses are likely to elicit either a neutral reaction—a shrugged "I'm sorry"—or a defensive retort: "It's not my fault you lack a sense of humor." Neither provides a bridge to further understanding. So save the strong response for what is really offensive.

For lesser breaches, Molly advises using your pushback as a point of engagement. For example: "To me, what you said this morning felt inappropriate. I'm telling you this because I know you're a good guy and don't want to make others uncomfortable. What are your thoughts?"

As Molly notes, this tack can be successful for several reasons. You are not making a characterization, you are simply sharing *how it felt to you*, which leaves room for other interpretations. Also, you are implicitly inviting the other person to be part of the solution.

If we make the decision not to offer feedback on a quip gone wrong, we want to avoid writing the other person off because in our view he or she failed at being funny. We all miscalculate, misjudge our audience, or simply blow it. We all say things we wish we could take back. So it's unrealistic and usually unfair to judge someone based on a single misinformed word or a perception.

An old saying attributed to an actor on his deathbed says it all: "Dying is easy. Comedy is hard."

WHEN WE FLOP

Sometimes we realize in the moment that our own attempts at humor are not landing with the light touch we intended. When this happens, the wisest course is to immediately acknowledge it. An apology—quick and sincere, not dragged out or overdone—is usually a good idea.

Adding a do-over can be even better.

Naomi Bagdonas and Jennifer Aaker share another great example. A former client of theirs, the founder of a media company, had worked with the same executive team for many years. When one member began to flounder, the team tried frank conversations, attempts at course correction, and coaching. But after a year, the consensus was that Mary had to go.

Mary had originally been scheduled to lead the team meeting that followed her departure, a task that now fell to the founder. Feeling nervous, he walked into the room and immediately joked, "Take it away, Mary!"

The air left the room. Everyone looked at one another. Then one team member spoke up: "I don't think that's funny."

The founder immediately agreed, saying he'd felt self-conscious about Mary's absence and was lamely attempting to defuse the tension.

"Let me try it again," he suggested, and left the room for a moment. On returning, he said, "Good morning, everyone. I know we have a lot to talk about today. But I want to open things up by saying a few words about Mary's departure, because I know it's been difficult for all of us."

The CEO had erred by being insensitive to the reaction his flippancy might provoke, so a bit more self-awareness would have saved him. But immediately accepting criticism when called out for his misfire, and then having the wit to restart the meeting, created a way for the team to move forward.

This story also underlines the value of pausing to ask yourself *Why do I want to say this?* whenever you're tempted to share a zinger. If your sole rationale is "because I think it's funny"—or, as in the case of this executive just cited, because you feel awkward—you might want to save it for the shower. That's one place where your stand-up routine will always be a hit.

CHAPTER NINE

Trigger 8: Attraction, the Uncomfortable Bits

We rise together by acknowledging the role
attraction can play in workplace relationships

The MeToo movement brought into the open a fundamental difference in how women and men have traditionally experienced the workplace. Even women who have not been personally targeted know harassment exists, and are familiar with grapevine warnings about who to avoid being alone with. So the revelations about powerful men who've harassed or assaulted women they've worked with, while disturbing and infuriating, did not come as a shock.

Men, by contrast, were often stunned when the news about prominent male leaders began making lurid headlines in 2017, continuing at a steady pace ever since.

The gulf between male and female perceptions was vividly illustrated by the *Washington Post*'s Dana Milbank in a profoundly honest column on the subject. Milbank wrote that his initial response to the headlines had been to marvel that "I'd spent my entire career in charmed workplaces where things like this never happened."

His innocence was shattered when a close female friend from one of those charmed workplaces filed a complaint against a powerful editor with whom Milbank had worked, exposing him as a serial and flagrant sexual predator. This was followed by revelations about a high-profile pundit at a news venue where Milbank had also been employed who turned out to be notorious for preying upon junior women.

How, Milbank wondered, could all this have happened right under his nose, without his having the least awareness?

His cluelessness felt especially galling since as a young writer Milbank had himself been bullied by these same men, though that harassment took a nonsexual form. Instead of being pinned against a sink in the washroom, he'd endured snide attacks on his work, been frozen out of key meetings, and been routinely denigrated as short of the mark.

These experiences were unpleasant and humiliating, but Milbank had viewed the men who treated him with aggressive disdain simply as guys who enjoyed throwing their weight around. And because these men held real power, he'd made a conscious decision to put up with their mistreatment in hopes of securing a ticket into the boys' clubs that ran their magazines. By implicitly agreeing to affirm these honchos' dominance—by not contesting their power or even defending himself—he'd sought to smooth his path into their inner circle.

The disclosures occasioned in response to MeToo made clear to Milbank that his female colleagues had been in no position to make similar trade-offs. The physical and sexual nature of the bullying they'd endured, along with the explicit threats, had far more damaging consequences for their psyches, their careers, and their lives. Recognizing this spurred his determination to do a better job of listening to and supporting female colleagues so he could stand with them against workplace abuse. Thousands of men I have spoken with over the last few years have shared similar sentiments.

Of course, sexual harassment is not just an issue for women. It impacts a range of sexual identities because the trigger of attraction is not binary. Men, especially those who are young, may be sexually harassed by men who hold positions of power, or by female predators, though this is far less common. And LGBTQ people are often the targets of comments that run the gamut from insulting to threatening.

NEW TERRAIN

By unsettling long-established patterns that thrived on female silence and male obliviousness, MeToo has mobilized support for policies aimed at bringing harassment into the open and penalizing those who dish it out, regardless of target. This hugely positive and ongoing process is having a profound impact on the workplace, and promises to make it fairer, safer, and more professional.

But by eroding the line between what has long been viewed as private—sexual behavior—and what is considered public—our lives as professionals and citizens—the global spread of MeToo has created a volatile environment in which perceptions about what is acceptable and what is not are routinely contested and constantly in flux. This can make it difficult to distinguish harassment from more benign forms of behavior in which attraction may—or may only seem—to play a role.

And so we all fumble for answers.

Are compliments acceptable? Are we allowed to ask whether someone is married? Could an invitation to lunch or, if we are traveling, to dinner, be misinterpreted? And what if we find ourselves drawn to a colleague, client, or customer? Is there a way to convey it appropriately, without giving rise to a complaint? What if we've been in a relationship with someone at work that we want to break off? Might that person retaliate by claiming that we engaged in predatory behavior?

Having to constantly negotiate such questions can keep us on guard and buttoned up. We may find ourselves second-guessing even trivial remarks and avoiding potential alliances or friendships out of concern that we, or others, could be misunderstood. This makes it tough to foster the kind of easy camaraderie required for work to be not just productive but enjoyable and engaging. And it makes it difficult to build trust.

This is an issue for companies and policy makers, but also for us as individuals. We need a sense of balance and clarity about what's potentially harmful and what most likely is not so we can better assess when to let go and when to take action.

GETTING PERSONAL

Compliments, for example, can spur confusion.

I recently worked with a midsized company headed by its founder, a man in his late sixties with a long history of hiring and promoting women. Arriving at the office one morning, Faizi found himself sharing the elevator with a recent hire, Robin, who was just a few years out of college. He noticed that she'd just had her long hair cut very short and, after greeting her, he smiled. "Great haircut."

That afternoon, Robin and two of her female colleagues paid him a visit. "Faizi, we thought it was better to come to you first instead of going to HR," said one colleague. "It's about the comment you made this morning."

"What comment? I'm not sure what you mean."

"Your comment about Robin's haircut. It's not appropriate to talk about a woman's appearance. You crossed a line."

Faizi was astonished and said he'd meant no harm.

"You wouldn't have told a *man* you liked his haircut," said Robin.

"Maybe not, because I probably wouldn't have noticed. Though if his hair had been really long, I might have. But where is this coming from? I've always given people compliments."

Robin's defender spoke up. "Things have changed. Compliments can get taken the wrong way. We know you're a good guy, so we wanted to let you know."

Faizi said he appreciated their coming to him, but continued to press the issue. "Are you suggesting I can't compliment anyone who works for me?"

Again, Robin's defender spoke: "Not a woman, and not if it relates to her appearance. It's too personal."

Faizi said fine and told Robin he was sorry he'd upset her. But speaking later with a friend, he remained baffled. "I didn't know a *haircut* was now considered personal. And withholding compliments seems like a poor way to boost morale. Plus how are we supposed build relationships if we can never say anything that's not directly work-related?"

Faizi and Robin's impasse demonstrates a downside of McToo's generally positive impact. Attempts to penalize warmth and spontaneity serve neither men nor women. Unilaterally declaring new rules can feel alienating and self-righteous. And being quick to do so primarily demonstrates a lack of trust.

So what's the alternative?

One key to dealing with situations like this is to start by assuming positive intent. For example, we can frame an occasional compliment as evidence that a colleague supports us and, however awkwardly, is trying to make us feel good. Our response in this case? Always a simple thank-you.

Of course, if the comments become habitual or take on sexual overtones ("I like the way that blouse fits you"), we need to address it with speed. It may be enough to say simply, "Your compliments are making me uncomfortable. Please stop." If the comments then continue, we'll know that good will is not a factor. We can enlist help from a trusted coworker, or take the issue to HR.

The subtext of Faizi and Robin's exchange was of course the notion that because he liked her haircut, he found her attractive, although in this case that was not what motivated his comment. Nevertheless, in a sensitized environment, we are encouraged to be wary, even fearful, of attraction. And to perceive it as necessarily disrespectful and out of bounds.

This is not especially helpful, given that attraction is a normal, even evolutionary, component of human life, a bedrock component of our nature. Trying to build a workplace in which attraction plays no role is not feasible. Devising realistic ways to address it is our best course.

TRANSPARENCY

While MeToo highlighted a fundamental difference in how men and women experience work, it also leveled the ground in one significant way. In the past, workplace romance tended to boomerang on women, while men—especially men who held positional power—were likely to get a pass. The exposure of a relationship with a coworker, boss, or client often resulted in a woman having to leave her job, while the man continued on with few consequences.

This has changed. The exposure of a workplace relationship or the aftermath of a breakup can now blow up a man's career as easily as a woman's, assuring that the trigger of attraction remains a disruptive force. HR can play a key role by formulating policies that can minimize the impact this trigger can have on all of our professional lives. But we as individuals need policies as well.

To start with, transparency is essential. No matter what the consequences, failing to be honest about what is going on is an invitation to disaster. The highly publicized case of Jeff Zucker, former president of CNN Worldwide, made this vividly clear.

A popular leader, Zucker had maintained a long-term relationship with the CMO of the company. Both were divorced, there was no egregious age or power disparity, nor any suggestion that either favoritism or harassment had been involved. The relationship was regarded as an open secret within the company; later news reports quoted coworkers as saying that "everybody knew." Yet neither Zucker nor his partner followed the corporate guidelines that mandated they report their relationship.

Their choice was not unusual. For example, a survey of employees conducted by the human resources platform Namely found that 70 percent of employees fail to report violations of company codes on harassment to their firm's HR team.

Yet in the wake of alleged misconduct involving CNN newsman Chris Cuomo's efforts to support his governor-brother during the latter's own sexual harassment scandal, the board of CNN's parent company concluded it had no choice but to fire Zucker—not for conducting an office romance, but for failing to disclose it. As a leader, the board reasoned that Zucker was responsible for setting a good example. Instead, he had openly flouted company policy. Some time later, Chris Cuomo was also fired.

This case made clear that transparency is now essential for everyone, without regard to positional power.

WHEN IT'S US

Yet reminding ourselves that "it's not the crime, it's the cover-up" that gets us into trouble doesn't make disclosing a relationship that our employer might view as problematic less difficult. Especially given that taking the actions called for in corporate guidelines may cost us our job, or result in an unwanted transfer.

Formally reporting a relationship may also be unappealing because it requires us to assess whether things have become serious enough to warrant such a step. Do we envision spending the rest of our life with this person? Does the other person envision this as well? And are we even ready to have that conversation? This conundrum is especially daunting because reporting is best done early in a relationship, which is precisely when we feel least ready to do so and least sure about how the relationship will unfold.

Elizabeth Spiers, former editor of the *New York Observer*, faced this dilemma when she realized she was falling in love with a co-worker who ran the company's commercial real estate trade publication and with whom she worked closely.

They had only had one date when Spiers concluded that, if they intended to continue seeing each other, they would need to report the relationship right away. She says, "Believe me, this is a discussion you *never* want to have at the start of a second date. Something along the lines of, are we serious enough about this to jeopardize our jobs by reporting it?"

Spiers was profoundly realistic. "I knew that, as Jotham's boss, I was potentially a walking sexual harassment lawsuit. It didn't matter that I had not harassed him; I was his boss, so that power differential created the opportunity. And I knew enough about labor law to be certain that there is *no* scenario in which you can date a subordinate and not be at risk of a sexual harassment lawsuit. Or a discrimination lawsuit if you promote or demote them."

An awkward conversation, to say the least, but Spiers is right. If it's love, we need to assess the potential costs and decide if we're prepared to face the consequences.

A BALANCING ACT

But what if it's not love? What if it's an intrigue, a flirtation, a fling? What if it's a way to add spice to our lives, a private little drama that gives us energy and (let's face it) spurs our interest in showing up for work? Aren't dreary conversations with HR antithetical to the let's-enjoy-it-while-it-lasts spirit of romance?

Our reservations will be especially strong if the secrecy, whispers, and little subterfuges are part of the spice. As a psychologist whose former husband proved to be a serial on-the-job philanderer observed, "Part of the thrill for him was the game, the intrigue, the knowledge that he was getting away with something. Being transparent would have spoiled the fun." How can you feel you're giving rein to your inner naughtiness if you're downloading disclosure forms or confessing all to your boss?

To be clear, we are not talking here about abusive relationships. We are talking about the trigger of mutual attraction, which has always been easily activated in the workplace. After all, we spend long hours with colleagues and often share fraught, emotionally draining, or joyfully triumphant moments while collaborating in pursuit of common goals. And given the increasing demands of work, how else are we supposed to meet people? Must dating apps be our only choice if we're single?

No, but especially with flirtations, it pays to know the potential costs so we can maintain our ability to consider the big picture, which includes what we really want from life and what we believe we can contribute to the world. It's also helpful to bear in mind that being attracted to someone does not mean we are impelled to act on that attraction. We can feel it, enjoy it, and just let it be.

This may sound counterintuitive to anyone raised in a culture that equates being true to our feelings with living life to the fullest. But refusing to heed our head as well as our heart when confronted by the emotional pull of attraction at work can lead us into trouble we are not prepared for.

It's also important to recognize that attraction often has an urgency that makes it *feel* important. Whereas in the larger scheme of things we often look back and see that what seemed important at a given moment was in retrospect merely urgent.

Keeping this in perspective and being clear about our larger priorities may be the last thing we feel like doing when urgency is upon us. But it beats allowing what ultimately may prove to be a passing impulse, what the French call a *folie à deux*, to spin our professional lives out of control.

SELF-RESPECT

Balancing head and heart, retaining the ability to demonstrate warmth and spontaneity without stirring the pot, is the true balancing act of our era. Maintaining this balance requires finding a midpoint between the opposing poles of acting out and repression in a way that suits our individual temperament and supports our goals.

How do we achieve this?

It starts with knowing ourselves, which means having a clear understanding of both our intentions and our capacity for risk. Knowing ourselves also requires that we recognize and accept our feelings as they arise, even as we keep our priorities in mind. Being able to hold conflicting impulses in equilibrium gives us power because it enables us to both draw upon and manifest self-respect.

Joan Didion's timeless essay "On Self-Respect" is useful here. Didion roots self-respect in our capacity to take our own measure and accept the potential consequences of our actions, including the risk that a relationship "may not turn out to be one in which *every day is a holiday because you're married to me.*"

She writes, "There is a common superstition that self-respect is a kind of charm against snakes, something that keeps those who have it locked in some unblighted Eden, out of strange beds, ambivalent conversations and trouble in general. It does not at all. It has nothing to do with the face of things, but concerns instead a private reconciliation."

Didion goes on to contrast two fictional characters: "the careless, suicidal Julian English in *Appointment in Samarra* and the careless, incurably dishonest Jordan Baker in *The Great Gatsby*." Jordan Baker, unlike Julian English, calculates the risks of her decisions and accepts that specific actions might come with specific costs. This enables her to have "the courage of her mistakes."

People with self-respect, says Didion, have precisely this courage because "They know the price of things. If they choose to commit adultery, they do not then go running, in an access of bad conscience, to receive absolution from the wronged parties; nor do they complain of the unfairness, the undeserved embarrassment, of being named co-respondent. In brief, people with self-respect exhibit a certain toughness, a kind of moral nerve; they display what was once called character, a quality which, although approved in the abstract, sometimes loses ground to other, more instantly negotiable virtues . . . Yet character—the willingness to accept responsibility for one's own life and actions—is the source from which self-respect springs."

To have character, Didion observes, "is potentially to have everything: the ability to discriminate, to love, and to remain indifferent. To lack it is to be locked within oneself, paradoxically incapable of either love or indifference."

Understanding this, and knowing what we are prepared to accept and what we are prepared to lose, will help us negotiate the confusions of an era in which the lines between our private and our public lives have eroded. This is now as true for men as it is for women, as true for straight people as it is for those who identify as LGBTQ.

THE RULES

Addressing the trigger of attraction requires us to understand our priorities and establish rules for ourselves. But advice from experts can also be helpful. Writing in the *Harvard Business Review*, Amy Gallo surveyed a range of psychologists and policy experts on the subject of office romance and came up with a concise list of dos and don'ts.

Here's a summary:

THE DOS

- Do know the risks involved, including potential conflicts of interest, reputational peril, and the chance that the relationship won't work out.
- Do accept that people may question your professionalism or your ability to succeed on your own merits.
- Do examine your intentions and question whether your feelings may be serving your own needs—for ego gratification, excitement, or getting ahead.
- Do know your company's policies thoroughly and understand the rationale behind them.
- Do "come clean early" if you have violated any regulations.
- Do talk through with a potential partner what each of you will do in the event that the relationship doesn't work out.

THE DON'TS

- Don't hide your relationship either by subterfuge or misdirection—people will always figure it out.
- Don't subject others to your relationship by acting unprofessionally in the presence of your partner.
- Don't pursue a coworker if you're not serious about a relationship.
- Don't date someone to whom you report, or who reports to you—just don't.
- Don't imagine that your special talents or position will earn you an exemption from any of these rules.

The trigger of attraction is challenging because of its volatile nature, and because its roots lie deep our psyches. Addressing it requires doing precisely what the present environment makes most difficult: giving others the benefit of the doubt; being direct and transparent, even when it feels uncomfortable; and distinguishing the sexualized abuse of power from everyday attraction, which is a normal expression of human nature.

PART II

A Culture of Belonging

CHAPTER TEN

The Power of Inclusive Behaviors

We rise together by practicing inclusive habits on a daily basis

Behaviors determine culture because culture lives in the details of how we do things. Yet although organizations have been exalting inclusion in mission statements and rolling out inclusion initiatives for the last twenty-five years, they've rarely put the focus on behaviors.

Instead, they routinely conflate inclusion with diversity, and so limit the scope of its application. Or they imagine that simply using the right words will brand them as an inclusive place to work.

I happen to know something about these efforts because *The Web of Inclusion*, which I've quoted several times in earlier chapters, was the first book to use the word *inclusion* in a business context.

I settled upon the image of a web because its structure mirrored the networked architecture of technology that was then evolving and would soon reconfigure how work is done. As an organizational structure, the web offered an alternative to the traditional hierarchies that had long dominated the workplace and that reflected a very different technological model. And because webs are organic, taking their shape from the natural world, I believed they had the potential to return work to a more human scale.

But a web of inclusion is not simply a structure. It is also a way of operating. As such, webs depend upon, enable, and reward the practice of inclusive behaviors and habits. This sets webs in opposition to the top-down style that previously prevailed in organizations. Instead of chains of command and communication channels determined by pecking order, webs spin tendrils of connection that enable people to communicate across levels and silos.

The Web of Inclusion had a fair amount of influence. Nearly thirty years later, I still get invited to speak on the subject, almost always as part of a diversity and inclusion initiative. This in itself says something about how the notion of inclusion has been absorbed into the fabric of organizations. Instead of permeating the culture, inclusion has gotten siloed, often viewed primarily as a tool for engaging women and others from outside the dominant leadership group, rather than a leadership skill that needs to be practiced at every level.

I had no thought of inclusion becoming yoked to diversity when *The Web of Inclusion* was published, although in the decades since the words *diversity* and *inclusion* (D&I) have become reflexively joined. The pairing makes sense given that individuals who have been underrepresented are more likely to perceive themselves as excluded, struggle to attract support, and be underrecognized for their potential.

The global spread of D&I (now DEI) initiatives and departments over the last twenty-five years has sought to rectify this situation. Yet the relationship between diversity and inclusion is often misunderstood.

For example, I frequently hear leaders describe diversity as their "goal." This makes little sense. Diversity is not an aspiration or an objective, it is a reality: it defines the nature of the global talent pool from which organizations large and small must draw. Inclusion by contrast is the only sustainably useful method for leading people who have historically stood outside the mainstream.

So diversity describes the *nature* of the situation, while inclusion describes the *means* by which the situation can most effectively be managed and led.

These are so often confused that I'm going to repeat this.

Diversity describes the *nature* of the situation, while inclusion describes the *means* by which the situation can most effectively be managed and led.

BEHAVIORS VERSUS BIASES

Despite having been frequently siloed, DEI initiatives often provide outsized value to organizations, especially those that tie them to mentoring circles, sponsorship, and coaching. Their primary weakness, in my experience and as I mentioned briefly in the introduction, has been their frequent reliance on unconscious bias training.

These trainings often start with employee surveys designed to reveal patterns of bias. The results are then used to design workshops or retreats in which participants are coached to acknowledge and name their own unconscious assumptions and prejudices, often in a group setting. The idea is that, through the simple process of recognition, people will begin to shift their behavior. It's basically a cathartic model, similar to those popularized by encounter groups, group therapy, and 12-step programs, in which we are presumed to benefit by telling on ourselves.

Rolling out unconscious bias training helps leaders feel they are doing something to help address often painful issues of diversity, equity, and inclusion. Yet the results are often disappointing. Over the years, I've spoken with too many clients who've undertaken costly initiatives, often on a global scale, which evaluations later showed had made little difference. Author and NYU professor of journalism Pamela Newkirk has extensively documented the ineffectiveness of much unconscious bias training in her groundbreaking book *Diversity, Inc.*

When I ask clients why they believe such efforts have failed to "move the needle" (a common observation), they usually cite small-bore specifics. The trainers weren't very good. Participants didn't dig down deep enough. Leadership didn't get behind the effort. There were too many introverts in the session.

By contrast, my experience, as well as Newkirk's research, suggests that the issue is more fundamental.

For starters, let's look at the term unconscious bias. What do the words tell us?

- They tell us that we are dealing with our *unconscious*, those random thoughts and impressions that float through our minds and exist outside our conscious control.
- They tell us that we are focusing on what is negative about ourselves: narrow, reactive, judgmental, limited, self-serving, embarrassing, potentially unkind—that is, our *biases*.

By definition, then, unconscious bias training asks participants to deal with negative material that lies outside their conscious control.

These trainings also, again by definition, focus on talk rather than action.

The guiding idea seems to be that having conversations will change us, uncomfortable conversations above all. But this is often untrue. As humans, we are more likely to change as the result of taking different actions that result in our having different experiences. These experiences then organically begin to shift our thoughts and perceptions.

In other words, *changing our actions is more likely to change our thoughts than changing our thoughts is to change our actions*.

Every one of us has probably experienced this.

For example, we think we don't like someone, but we make an effort to treat them well, and they respond positively to our effort. We are then more likely to start liking them based on their response to our positive efforts than by arbitrarily deciding that we *should* be more open to that person. Simply recognizing our biases does not give us an intuitive path forward, whereas taking action does.

Also, it doesn't really matter to someone else if negative thoughts about them occasionally float through our minds. What matters is that we treat them with appreciation and respect. Our behaviors are what make the difference, not our random unstated thoughts. Which are, let's be honest, nobody's business.

The unconscious bias approach can also stir up defenses and activate triggers, as we saw with Alex, the engineer, in Chapter 6. That's in part because unconscious bias training privileges certain kinds of bias over others. Women can more easily get away with making negative generalizations about men, while people of color may get a pass for observing that "white people always . . . (fill in the dots)." This hierarchy of resentment and perception is historically understandable. Yet encouraging people to be honest about their negative perceptions in a group setting can result in increased division and stir backlash—which is exactly what happened with Alex.

Certainly, these programs do some good. The surveys provide useful information. Individuals may have aha moments or epiphanies as they recognize how an attitude formed early in life undermines their ability to form positive relationships with certain colleagues. Yet unconscious bias is often a scattershot, unsure, and potentially counterproductive method for organizations, teams, units, or divisions seeking to create a culture in which the greatest possible number of people feel as if they belong.

NEW WAYS OF BEING

Instead, I'd like to propose a positive and action-based approach. One that enables us to live our way into a new way of thinking rather than attempting to think our way into a new way of being.

It starts with clearly articulating specific practices that any one of us can use to create cultures of belonging. These practices are useful for us as individuals, no matter how senior or junior we are. They are also helpful for teams and organizations seeking to break down barriers, levels, and boundaries so that people can communicate and collaborate more broadly.

These practices include but are not limited to those described as follows.

ACTIVE LISTENING

At least two books on leadership cross my desk each week. Invariably, they include a chapter or section headed with the imperative "Listen!"

Of course, listening—attempting to discipline our distracting thoughts so we can really hear and consider what another person is saying—is important (indeed imperative) as far as it goes. But creating an inclusive culture requires something more. Listening on its own is a mental discipline, an internal process. Unless we also *demonstrate* that we are listening, others may not feel heard.

Building on What Previous Speakers Say

There are few more powerful ways of making others feel heard than referencing points they have made in our remarks during a meeting, brainstorming session, or in conversation. We know this because we've all experienced the glow when someone has shown this generosity to us by noting, "I'm going to build on what Anne said" or "I agree with Bashir's observation." We often feel unreasonably grateful to whoever does this because it lets us know that we've been heard.

It's therefore smart to take every genuine opportunity that comes our way to relate the points we make to what others have said. And to spread the love broadly rather than just building on remarks by those who hold more senior positions, which, done on a regular basis, will mostly succeed in making us look like suck-ups.

What holds us back from following this simple policy?

Often it's simply that we haven't fully heard what others are saying, either because we're preoccupied with what *we* intend to say, or we're in the habit of letting our minds wander. These are typical symptoms of undisciplined listening.

Another reason we fail to build on what others say is that we may rely too heavily on prepared remarks, bullet points, and slides, especially during meetings. This can trap us into sticking rigidly with our script. We pour forth information instead of viewing get-togethers as an opportunity for real exchange.

In this way, overscripted meetings undermine our ability to build more inclusive cultures. Yet they remain a feature in teams and organizations. As an alternative, we can always send bullet points or slides to participants in advance of a meeting, requesting that they think them through before the discussion.

This approach is obvious but often overlooked, especially by those who rely heavily on prepared remarks. Yet few experiences are less inspiring than sitting through a meeting in which people attempt to make relevant comments or share their responses while the speaker keeps clicking along: "Good point, but we've got to get through these slides."

Really? Must we?

If we instead consider every meeting as an opportunity to build consensus, cohesion, and a sense of belonging in addition to sharing information, we will see the futility of prefab presentations.

Avoiding Overconfirmation

Building on a colleague's points will benefit no one if our efforts seem intrusive. But this is what happens when we try to demonstrate that we are listening by constantly confirming: *good point, terrific, yes!* It may feel to us as if we're showing empathy and being a good listener. But if we do it repeatedly, it breaks the flow.

I learned this the hard way, back in the pre-virtual era when delivering a group coaching to twenty managers in a large insurance company. The meeting was scheduled to be in-person, but eight participants from one site got caught in a snowstorm and had to dial in by phone. The exchange, which was lively, was audio recorded, and I was eager to hear the tape because I'd been too busy coaching to take any notes. Yet hearing the tape felt agonizing because every time someone said anything, I heard myself interrupting: *What a terrific idea! I agree! I hadn't thought of that!* It was not only irritating, repetitive, and overly perky, but after the first few times, it began to sound as if I were trying to hijack the meeting, making it all about me and my responses.

The perils of overconfirmation have only become more pressing in our virtual environment. For example, if we're on a platform like Zoom and our microphone is on, the technology automatically spotlights us every time we affirm what anyone says. We've all seen this happen: a person who's extremely empathic or enthusiastic ends up repeatedly grabbing the screen as they eagerly try to signal their support. The effect is disruptive, the very opposite of what they intend.

Speaking Last

Peter Drucker was probably the most influential management thinker of the twentieth century, and a remarkable person to spend time with. He radiated knowledge and wisdom but was also a highly engaged listener. You knew you were in the presence of a giant.

Peter had a rule for himself: he was always the last to speak. Whether it was a one-on-one or a big meeting, he waited until everyone had finished before he weighed in. By doing so, he demonstrated discipline, patience, and humility. But this practice also had specific benefits.

First, it avoided the danger that other people would adjust or adapt what they had to say because they had been influenced by what he had said. This is an issue for anyone in a senior position: once you've spoken, others tend to fall into line and any questions, concerns, or objections they might have raised remain unspoken as they trip over themselves to agree with you. This deprives you of information while assuring that others don't feel heard, even though they're the ones who've chosen to self-censor.

Speaking last also gives you the opportunity to think through what others have shared, increasing the likelihood that your responses will be relevant. And it gives you the chance to build upon what previous speakers say because you've had a chance to hear them. Waiting gives you time to both listen and demonstrate that you're listening. And as Peter recognized, it augments your own authority. You get to sum things up, and perhaps suggest a path forward.

ENGAGING ACROSS LEVELS AND DIVISIONS

How you listen matters, but *who* you listen to does as well.

Innovative or strategic ideas often percolate among those who lack the positional power to put their insights into practice but whose frontline experience connects them directly with customers and clients and whose hands-on work alerts them to potential product or service glitches. Yet their valuable, experience-based insights often go unshared with those who make top-level decisions for the simple reason that frontline people are rarely in the room when these decisions are discussed.

This is how the American auto industry famously operated before it was nearly put out of business by Japan, whose integrated manufacturing model was the polar opposite of the US's top-down model. When a US manufacturer had a problem with poorly fitting doors, leadership typically did not seek answers from assembly line workers whose job was actually fitting those doors onto cars. Although these workers were a repository of information that the company could have used to minimize defects and so stanch the flow to Japanese vehicles, they were not solicited for insights.

But those were the bad old days, right? The days when communication was almost entirely top-down and siloed hierarchies didn't speak across rigid lines. Yes, of course. But while decades of cautionary tales about manufacturing and marketing meltdowns have given silos a bad name and leaders today have learned to speak the language of inclusion, their efforts are often restricted to the redesign of management charts or the appointment of ombudsmen to convey information across traditional divides. What's needed instead are simple practices that enable people at every level to share ideas, observations, and concerns.

One way to ensure cross-barrier communication is to regularly invite a range of people to participate in key meetings. The people who pick up the phones, sell the products, repair what's broken, and handle customer complaints are a resource whose embedded knowledge needs to be heard.

The Details Matter

The most frequent objection to including frontline people is that they may be reluctant to speak up because they feel intimidated or are unaccustomed to being heard. Yet this is most likely to occur when the details of a meeting aren't managed in a way that encourages contribution.

For example, the CEO of a midsize Phoenix-based consulting company was eager to break down its traditionally formal culture. The previous leadership team had pretty much communicated only among themselves or with their direct reports. To shake things up, the new CEO began routinely including a range of people in every strategy session. Yet he was disappointed at participation levels and wondered if he was doing something wrong.

The employees knew exactly where the problem lay.

Said Trefana, a recent hire in the company's commercial lines department, "I couldn't believe it when my boss asked me to attend the leadership team's monthly strategy meeting. Me, sitting in the same conference room as the CEO! My boss let me know that I'd be expected to give some feedback or make observations based on my contact with clients, so I came prepared. But it felt strange because the senior team was seated around this big table with their direct reports right behind them and everyone else bunched up in back. If I said anything, it would have forced the senior people to turn around, which made speaking up feel like a really big deal. Since no one called on me, I didn't volunteer. I learned later that my boss was disappointed."

This is not atypical. A leader committed to breaking down silos calls a meeting that looks beyond the usual suspects to include people from different levels and divisions. Yet strict hierarchical protocols about who sits where and who speaks first remain in place. These are often maintained out of concern that senior people will take it amiss if they're relegated to "Siberia," or not invited to respond first. Yet these concerns primarily demonstrate that the commitment to inclusive practices has not penetrated beyond the leadership team.

Research confirms that employees are likely to perceive their executive team as more committed to inclusion than those one level down, and those one level down as more committed than those two levels down—and so on in descending order. Given this, and since most peoples' experience of their organization is primarily shaped by interactions with their direct boss, it's little wonder that well-intentioned efforts to break down levels of privilege and operate as one team are often viewed in the ranks as being "all talk." People hear the CEO speaking eloquently about his commitment and read glowing statements on the company's website, but they don't *feel* the impact in their day-to-day work.

This is what happened at the consulting firm's strategy meeting. The executive team was fully committed to the changes they were trying to put in place and assumed their senior people would go along, but they kept seating protocols in place as a way of placating those who might not yet be fully onboard. This decision guaranteed they would send a mixed message when the company opened the session to a range of employees.

SHOWING HOW IT'S DONE

One benefit of including people at different levels in key meetings is that it gives younger employees the chance to see for themselves how senior jobs are done. Rather than being presented with a list of leadership dos and don'ts at a training session, they get to absorb their lessons by watching experienced leaders in action.

I got a good demonstration of this years ago while shadowing Frances Hesselbein, who was then CEO of Girl Scouts of the USA. At the time, Frances was routinely cited in such magazines as *BusinessWeek* and *Fortune* as one of the most skillful leaders in the world. This was unheard of for a nonprofit executive who worked with young girls.

One day, Frances had a scheduled call with a *New York Times* reporter to discuss a controversy about that year's Girl Scout cookies. She invited her entire six-person communications team to sit in on the call, including two recent hires in their midtwenties. When they arrived at her office, Frances welcomed them with tea and then proceeded to explain the specifics of what she hoped to accomplish with the reporter.

The team sat quietly through the long and at times challenging exchange, which Frances kept on speakerphone for their benefit. When the call concluded, she asked for questions and comments. When no one but the head of the team volunteered, Frances began asking individual team members what they'd noticed, what they'd learned, and why they thought she had handled various points in the way she had.

After they left, Frances noted the advantages of this approach. "The team I invited today is in communications, so they need to know how to deal with the press. But how can they learn that if they never see how it's done? Sitting in on a call like this is a good way to give them experience they can draw on when their time comes. In a lot of organizations, young people never get this kind of exposure. But it's always more effective to model leadership behaviors than teach them."

HONORING THE SQUEAKY WHEEL

A Houston-based aerospace firm struggling to retain female talent created a women's advisory council to help the senior team address the reluctance of talented women to stick around. Bethany, the HR head, issued a call for candidates to join the council. Nine women and two men volunteered.

As Bethany went over the list, her heart sank. "I was concerned about Flora," she said. "She's smart and a strong contributor, but she's not one of our most diplomatic employees and she's a flamethrower when it comes to women's advancement. My fear was that she could hijack the meetings with her concerns, or end up alienating others on the council."

Bethany was facing the common problem of what to do with a squeaky wheel: someone heavily invested in a particular cause who is known among coworkers for their advocacy and unafraid to speak their minds, often at length. These firebrands can make it tough for working groups to reach consensus. And at times, they can be a pain to work with.

Bethany's concern put me in mind of one of the key practices that made the *Miami Herald*'s fairness task force, described in Chapter 6, an unprecedented success. Dave Lawrence, the paper's publisher, who pulled the task force together, stated that one of its guiding principles must be to "honor the squeaky wheel." That is, the task force should actively seek to include those who were most adamant about specific challenges that the group wanted address.

Yes, Dave acknowledged, squeaky wheels often make meetings difficult to manage, dragging out the process and at times trying their colleagues' patience. But he pointed out that the time they consume on the front end, in the planning and consensus phase of an initiative, is often compensated for by the time they gain on the back end. This is true for the simple reason that whatever the squeaky wheels agree to is likely to get buy-in from skeptical colleagues.

Dave noted, "People think, if *Susan* signed off on this, it must be good for new hires because she's always going on about how this company operates like an exclusive club. That's the great hidden value of squeaky wheels: they're credibility builders. If you get them onboard, other people will believe you're serious about addressing an issue."

In Bethany's case, excluding Flora from the council would no doubt make the process smoother and signal that consensus and harmony were important. But since when do consensus and harmony characterize effective change? Change is notoriously messy, so prioritizing unruffled feathers tends to send a message that the company prefers to minimize disruption rather than seriously wrestling with the painful challenges it says it wants to address.

Bethany realized that sidelining Flora could result in the council producing a list of generic recommendations that did little to change the core issues driving women out of the company. By contrast, including Flora, and possibly pairing her with someone more senior, could build credibility among the very women Bethany had been tasked to retain, and so increase the likelihood that the council would achieve its purpose.

Taking Nothing Off the Table

One of Bethany's chief fears about Flora was that she'd urge the council to address promotion policies for those working flexible hours, which she viewed as a separate issue from the retention crisis. "If we bring in a whole slew of issues, I'm afraid we'll get bogged down," she lamented.

Again, the *Miami Herald*'s fairness initiative offers a template for dealing with the often-expansive range of concerns that trying to initiate inclusive practices often raises. Two of the squeaky wheels on the *Herald* task force continually harped on the company's parking policies, which assigned lot spaces in accordance with rank. Senior leaders were assured of the best spots regardless when (or if) they arrived, while "we peons" had to park far from the building, even when arriving at six a.m. with armloads of documents to lug to the office.

The task force leaders at first objected: "It's not our job to look at parking. Our purpose is to make the *Herald* a fairer place." But of course, the paper's parking policies were viewed by those affected as profoundly unfair, symbolic of the company's perceived disregard for anyone who lacked positional power. Thanks to pressure from a few of the squeaky wheels, the task force ended up including revisions to parking policy in its list of recommendations.

Losing their prime parking spots was not what the *Herald*'s leadership had in mind when they signed off on the task force. Yet changing this one policy did more to convince employees that the paper was serious than any of the other actions they took. That's because the first thing people saw when they drove up to work each morning was tangible proof that the paper was becoming more fair.

DEMONSTRATING GENEROSITY

When we feel we're not valued, when we believe our contributions are ignored, we may react by shutting down. This can push us into a cynical mind-set that shapes our internal dialogue. "Nobody goes out of their way to help me. Why should I go out of my way to help other people?"

Indulging such thoughts undermines our ability to build relationships, depriving us of the kind of support we need to be able to assert our value. Instead, we dig down into a place of unhappiness, convinced that we have the moral high ground because we're simply responding to how we've been treated.

The most effective way to escape this trap is to act in a totally contrary spirit, going out of our way to make others feel good even when we're not feeling the love ourselves. This kind of willed generosity is exemplified by the Saint Francis prayer: "Let me seek to console rather than to be consoled, to understand rather than to be understood, to love rather than to be loved."

President Kennedy gave the sentiment a secular twist and inspired a whole generation when he exhorted, *Ask not what your country can do for you, ask what you can do for your country.*

We demonstrate generosity when we act without calculating reward or considering whether the object of our generosity deserves it. This is good for the world, but it's also good for us. It's the very definition of a win-win, as my colleague John Baldoni writes in his powerful book *Grace*, citing the role of generosity in creating circles of reciprocity that strengthen us even as we share—the very definition of rising together.

Generosity operates similarly to the practice of giving others the benefit of the doubt, as advocated throughout Part 1 of this book. John Baldoni also notes that giving this benefit—a form of unearned truth—is another way of manifesting grace. But generosity reframes this mental exercise by tying it to specific actions: small civilities, kind words, thoughtful gestures.

It's amazing, for example, how much pleasure we can generate by taking a moment to recognize another person, either verbally or by sending a quick text or note:

- "I loved what you said in that meeting."
- "I admire how you speak up."
- "Watching you helps me learn how to listen."
- "What you said just made my day!"

My colleagues Chester Elton and Adrian Gostick, known as the "Gurus of Gratitude," advise us to be lavish with our appreciation, even in difficult circumstances. Their most important tip: Give praise now, give it often, and don't be afraid or hold back.

But what if others don't seem to notice or appreciate our efforts? What if we still feel undervalued?

Unless we're getting a clear message to back off, our best course is usually to try again. Why? Because being generous ultimately helps us feel good about *ourselves*.

And why would we deprive ourselves of that opportunity?

INVESTING IN COLLEAGUES' CAREER DEVELOPMENT

There are few more effective ways to show generosity than by letting others know that we're committed to their success. We can do this at every level and stage of our career, without regard to barriers of gender, race, or age.

If We're Senior

If we hold a senior position, we can ask newer hires where they would like their job to lead. And rather than accepting vague responses, such as "I'm happy where I am" or "I haven't given it much thought," we can push them to spell out in specific terms about what they want from their careers. And we can invite them to keep us in the loop as their thinking evolves.

We can also ask people at less senior levels what skills or experience they may not be making use of, and then be on the lookout for opportunities for them to develop these talents. This is a simple way of assuring that people feel valued for their potential, rather than just for what they contribute. And it signals our willingness to serve them as an informal mentor.

I've conducted hundreds of confidential exit interviews over the years and find one of the most frequent reasons people (women especially) give for leaving is, "My company never understood what I could do," or "My boss had no idea of the things I could have been good at." So putting exploratory questions directly—"What talents do you have that I should know about?"—lessens the chance that our team members will feel undervalued and disconnected. This in turn helps us to better leverage their talents.

Another helpful line of inquiry is asking what someone needs in order to operate at their best. "How do you like to be managed? What kind of policies could help you make the most efficient use your time? What opportunities could help you develop relationships that might be useful to you in the future?" Questions like these are enormously helpful, not only to the junior people we ask, but for us as well. They enable us to be more skilled and effective managers and enhance our ability to get results.

If We're Junior

When we're in the early stages of our careers, we often take an exalted view of more senior people, failing to recognize that, even when they are generous and supportive, they are also invested in assuring their own success. We can benefit by acknowledging this and letting our managers know we understand that part of our job is helping *them* look good—to clients, customers, and those whom they report.

I often hear people complain that their boss takes credit for the work they do. But while it's wonderful when a manager goes out of his or her way to publicly call out a team member's contribution, it doesn't necessarily happen. The team leader or manager is responsible for the outcome and takes the weight for failure, so the team leader also gets bragging rights for success.

Therefore, when we accept a new assignment or role, we might start by asking our manager how we can do our job in a way that benefits them, while also helping the whole team to shine. Doing so signals our willingness to act as an ally who understands and values our boss's interests. This kind of "I have your back" message is an effective tool for building support across barriers and divides, as well as for defusing triggers. It shows that we get how things work, and that we're a potential player.

THE POWER OF NOMINATING

We often assume that only senior leaders can serve as sponsors because their connections and position give them the means to invest in colleagues of their choosing. They do so by advocating for others, recommending them for new positions, endorsing their skills, and promoting their interests. This may appear to us as one of the perks of power: being able to influence events by helping others to rise. But we don't need to wait until we hold a high position to do this. We can get active in sponsoring others at any point in our careers.

One of the most effective ways to do this is to nominate or recommend colleagues for honors, awards, and plum assignments. If we're on the lookout to do so, we'll find many opportunities. And if we're explicitly asked for recommendations, responding with enthusiasm rather than considering it an imposition—or worse, viewing the person making the request as self-serving—gives us a chance to build and extend our network in a positive way.

Recommending and endorsing not only helps our colleagues, it ultimately benefits us. Those for whom we do favors are more likely to reciprocate when we ask them to do the same for us. My colleague Ruth Gotian, who heads professional development at New York's Weill Cornell Medical Center and studies extremely high-performing individuals, talks about the impact this discovery had on her own development.

"It started when a very senior man in the medical world asked whether I would nominate him for an award," Ruth recalls. "I was surprised that someone at his level would want my help. But I was even more surprised because I hadn't realized that this is how things are done, that a person can *ask* others for this kind of endorsement. I guess I assumed that endorsements and honors just sort of happened. But he was very open about it and asked a ton of people. It was clear he wanted as many votes as he could get."

Ruth finds the assumption that endorsements "just happen" to be more common among women. "Men, especially men from dominant groups who understand how the system works and assume they're going to be successful, don't seem inhibited in making this kind of request. For women, it can be more complicated. We fear seeming pushy, or we worry that someone will see us as self-serving. But we can't afford to let that fear hold us back. Asking someone for help means they can ask *us* as well, which gives us the opportunity to pay it back, or pay it forward. And when we offer support *first*, it demonstrates confidence in our own ability to contribute, while also making the world a better place."

What particularly impressed Ruth was that the man who requested her endorsement made the process easy. "He gave me letters other people had written I could use as a model. He provided the language that would be most helpful to him. I didn't have to spend a lot of time trying to figure out what I should say, which had made me reluctant to do this kind of thing in the past. I decided I was going to learn from him and get active asking for help, making it easy for people to provide it, and offering to recommend other people. My relationships blossomed as a result."

HIRING TO MAKE IT HAPPEN

There are few more effective ways to build an inclusive organization than to prioritize inclusive skills when hiring. The power of this approach was brought home to me several years ago when I was working with an Asia-based natural resources company that was seeking to shift its culture, both at headquarters and in sites around the world. Their leadership was motivated not just by the desire to attract more diverse talent and burnish the company's image, but also by a newly discovered and compelling financial imperative.

The shift began when the recently installed CEO commissioned the company's first-ever survey of employees across the globe, from regions as diverse as Mongolia, South Africa, and Chile. This was unprecedented given the traditional, top-down engineering culture that had dominated the company since its founding, one in which employee views and opinions were not much regarded.

The consultants hired to develop the survey recommended four questions specifically related to perceptions of inclusion. These queries sought to learn the extent to which employees believed that their voices were heard and valued, and perceived that their expertise was factored into decisions that affected their work. The results of the survey were then delivered to an internal team drawn from across the company for analysis.

While combing through masses of data, a female engineer from Peru working on the project noticed that two of the sites where inclusion ranked lowest had recently reported safety problems. This inspired her to compare safety records at sites around the world with the survey results. In doing so, she found a direct correlation between perceptions of inclusion and site safety. Where people felt heard and valued, sites had excellent records. Where they did not, site records were poor.

Since profitability in mining can be catastrophically impacted by safety problems, and because companies with poor records can lose their license to operate in specific countries or regions, the data made a powerful financial case for more inclusive practices. Yet when the senior team launched a series of initiatives and policy changes, they ran into resistance from site supervisors and managers who viewed listening to their people as a sign of weakness and soliciting employee views as coddling.

So in addition to extensive retraining, the company decided to shift how it did its hiring to reflect the values it was trying to inculcate. While a degree from a top engineering school had previously been considered the chief qualification for a managerial position, the firm now began looking for people with experience in the safe delivery of human services: emergency workers, critical care nurses, EMTs, accident mitigation specialists. That is, people motivated by the desire to help others and accustomed to making decisions based on what they learned through inquiry and consultation.

The company, in essence, began hiring for inclusion.

Tom Peters, who has been studying and writing about excellence for the last forty years, sees this as a trend. He cites a home health care company he worked with that had been troubled by increasing hospitalization rates for people who could have been treated as outpatients if their condition had been identified earlier.

When the provider began interviewing clients to get a sense of what was going wrong, they found the primary problem was that their frontline people failed to ask the right questions, listen carefully to patient responses, and follow up on potentially useful information. Instead, they were focused on efficiencies and task completion. On asking questions just to check the boxes.

As a result of these findings, the provider decided to flip its recruiting practices and ask prospective hires about what community service they had done. The idea was that those who had volunteered in their communities were more likely to be caring and attentive to others. The provider then hired people with this kind of background to fill financial, operating, and medical positions.

Within a year, client hospitalizations decreased significantly.

Tom believes that "ninety percent of our problems could be ameliorated if we hired for collegiality. Instead, many organizations continue to recruit and promote people based on technical skills, presumed brilliance, charisma, and having the right connections. This is actually an effective way to *screen out* the kind of soft skills companies need to keep people motivated and engaged and to deliver superior customer and client service."

As Tom notes, while you can train for technical skills (which keep changing), it's harder to train for caring. "But you can hire for it. You want to look for people who relate to others, listen well, and do not condescend to or categorize those they work with. People who care create companies that care, so make sure your hiring reflects this. And remember that hot shots who enjoy lording it over others often have outsize and lasting effects."

AHA MOMENT: NOW WHAT?

Every one of us, no matter our level, can use the practices described in this chapter to help build more inclusive teams and cultures. But behavior-based approaches can be extraordinarily effective when a leader makes a wholehearted commitment to focusing on behavior, not bias.

Mike Kaufmann, until recently CEO of Cardinal Health, offers an example. Mike was so passionate about advancing women in his company that he only accepted invitations to deliver keynotes to outside groups if he could speak on topics relating to diversity, equity, and inclusion.

About fourteen years ago, Mike decided to work directly with Cardinal's women's employee resource group, then a new and relatively small network. This hands-on experience helped him better understand both what women could contribute and the cultural and structural constraints that held them back. As a consequence, he took two actions aimed at enabling him to more effectively champion women in the company and to increase female participation, especially at senior levels.

First, he hired an outside coach with decades of experience in women's leadership to work with him solely on gender issues. He says, "I needed someone who understood the challenges and knew what progress looked like. And who would tell me what I needed to hear instead of what I wanted to hear."

Second, he enlisted five to seven "truth tellers" from within Cardinal, internal people tasked with keeping him informed about the company's successes and setbacks in regard to women. He says, "I met with them regularly. After I gave a keynote, I questioned them. What did you think? How did that work? What could I have done better? I also asked them what was going on in the company, where there might be potential problems, and how what people said aligned with their behavior. These conversations helped me understand who was a good apple and who was a bad apple, who's working to improve things and who was not buying in. I didn't necessarily fire the bad apples—though I did do that. But I made sure whoever it was started acting in a way that supported what we were trying to do."

Two years ago, Mike expanded this approach to include race. He brought in an outside coach, an African American with long experience, who would tell him what he needed to hear. And he assembled five to seven internal truth tellers who meet with him regularly to give feedback on racial progress and roadblocks.

During the quarterly town halls Mike held for all employees, he always spent two hours on topics related to DEI. He engaged employees at every level to share personal stories, as individuals or on panels. These narratives spurred plenty of aha moments.

One such moment came during a town hall where a couple of hiring managers discussed the continuing reluctance of female employees to apply when a senior position became available. Several women joined in, describing why these situations made them hesitant and why they often believed they lacked the right qualifications.

Mike recognized that the company's hiring managers could benefit by building prospective job slates based not on who volunteered for new positions, but on who the manager believed were the most qualified candidates. Putting this idea into practice quickly resulted in more women being promoted.

Mike says, "I talked about this experience to an external group. Afterward, a CEO in pharma called to say that he'd been struck by my remarks. He was looking to appoint a new CFO and two men had put their names in the ring, but the woman he believed was most qualified had not. He'd been about to choose one of the men, but after hearing me, he told the woman he thought she'd make an ideal candidate. She said she appreciated the offer but then spent half an hour arguing with him, telling him all the reasons she wasn't ready for this kind of position."

Suddenly, says Mike, the CEO decided to stop arguing. "He told her he'd made up his mind. He believed she was as ready as anyone in the company and probably had more actual experience, so she was his choice. He later called to let me know that she had been so successful in her new position that he'd just been promoted to president of the company. He said it would never have happened if he hadn't heard my talk. That was his aha moment."

Mike notes that aha moments don't amount to much if they don't spur action and change behavior. So his personal motto, one he shares as widely as he can, has become *"Aha moment. Now what?"*

Talking with Mike, I realized that *Aha moment. Now what?* also describes the structure of this book.

The triggers described in Part 1 provide dozens of aha moments, while also identifying ways they can be addressed.

The inclusive practices described in this and the next chapters are devoted to *Now what*: actions we can take to move beyond barriers that keep our relationships stuck and hold us back from building cultures of belonging.

CHAPTER ELEVEN

Informal Enlistment

We rise together by enlisting one another's support

Building cultures of belonging sounds like an attractive and useful idea. And breaking it down into simple practices, such as speaking last, honoring the squeaky wheel, and investing in colleagues' development, makes it seem straightforward, even simple.

But just because it's simple doesn't mean it's easy.

One difficulty is that, as humans, we seem to come equipped with built-in forgetters. We resolve to do something in a healthier or more beneficial way, and we feel inspired or hopeful at the start. But after a few weeks or months, we hit a rough patch. Maybe we're tired, irritable, or discouraged. Or maybe we're just sick of the effort change requires. Under pressure, we default to our habitual responses and established behaviors. And in time, we forget what we've been working diligently to achieve.

Breaking any kind of habit is hard because defaulting to our comfort zone feels easy, familiar, and safe. By contrast, doing something in a new way requires us to think through our actions and responses. Our brains and neural systems read this as extra work and so register it as discomfort. If we're in the habit of speaking first, holding back feels awkward. If we usually avoid people we perceive as not our style, trying to connect with them can feel fake. If we're used to taking our seat at the back of the room, suddenly striding to the front row feels intrusive, even rude.

Please note: none of these actions is intrinsically awkward, inauthentic, or intrusive. They just *feel* that way because we're not accustomed to them. To sustain change, we need to tolerate feeling a bit uncomfortable until new habits get established. And we need to build structures of support that hold us accountable for what we're trying to achieve.

If we lack such support, our discomfort may spur us to devise narratives that serve as an excuse for reverting to established habits.

Narratives such as:

- *Why am I trying to talk with this person? We have so little in common!*
- *I feel like an idiot, pretending that I care.*
- *This meeting is just too boring—time for me to slip out.*
- *Why should I give up my seat to that dullard?*

Such thoughts are primed to undermine our efforts. That's their purpose: to nudge us back into our comfort zone so we can avoid the stress to our systems that change inevitably stirs. Pushing back requires us to subject our resistance to a reality check. That means getting out of our heads and enlisting support.

INFORMAL ENLISTMENT 101

Enlisting support gives us both perspective and a potential means for holding ourselves to account for the changes we seek to make. It also provides an additional incentive to persevere when change feels hard. If we've made a point of telling a colleague that we intend to practice a new behavior—especially if we've asked for their help—we're more likely to follow through because we don't want to look foolish.

Knowing we have support also helps to disable our built-in forgetter because seeing, or even thinking about, the person we have taken into our confidence reminds us that we have made a commitment to act in a different way.

Engaging others in our efforts to make positive behavioral changes is always a good idea. And there are many ways to do it. In my workshops and coaching, I use a simple practice I call informal enlistment. I adapted this technique from Marshall Goldsmith's Feedforward method—soliciting feedback aimed at future action rather than delivering a rearview mirror critique. It also draws on his Stakeholder Centered Coaching, which requires coachees to enlist colleagues' insights to help them grow.

Marshall developed these practices in response to research on what people who are able to sustain long-term positive behavioral change have in common. The answer? *They don't try to do it alone.* They work with a coach, a peer coach, or a mentor who gives suggestions, spurs them on, and holds them to account by following up.

Of course, not everyone can afford a coach, and many of us struggle to secure the right mentor. The advantage of informal enlistment is that it enables any one of us to adapt the don't-do-it-alone premise to our everyday circumstances. It is both simple and easy, requiring a minimal investment of time, and no financial cost. We don't even need to give it a lot of thought. We simply follow the steps, making adjustments as we go along.

There are two primary ways to practice informal enlistment. The first is soliciting real-time support. The second is situational peer coaching.

SOLICITING REAL-TIME SUPPORT

The most basic form of informal enlistment is soliciting support in advance of a meeting, a presentation, or any occasion where you plan to practice a new habit.

Say you're preparing an in-person presentation to your team. Shortly beforehand, you approach a colleague. Here's a possible script:

"I'd like to ask a favor of you ahead of the meeting we'll be in together this afternoon."

"What's that?"

"I'm going to be talking about how the new software rollout is working and I anticipate a lot of questions. I've had feedback that I get too detailed when I'm talking about technology and leave some people confused. Could you watch and let me know whether I get too much into the weeds? Or whether there's a place where I might have been clearer? I really need to get better at this and would be grateful for your thoughts."

"Sure, I can do that."

"Thanks! I'll check back after the meeting to hear what you have to say."

When you do check back, your only role is to listen. You don't comment, you don't explain why the suggestion you're being offered might not work. You don't promise to act on the advice you're being given in the future. *You just listen.*

And then, you say thank you again.

What could be simpler? But what could be more effective? Just look at all you've managed to accomplish:

- You've let your colleague know that you're working to get better at something, and so demonstrated your dedication, your diligence, and your humility.
- You've let her know that you value and respect her opinion and are eager to hear what she has to say.

- You've opened the door to a relationship based on a proactive show of trust by being honest and making yourself a bit vulnerable.
- You've positioned yourself to get some positive and helpful ideas that may make you better at your job and in your life.
- You've asked to be held accountable for taking action on a habit that's getting in your way, which increases the likelihood that you'll do so.
- You've leveraged a colleague in your own development.
- You've expanded your network in a positive way.

The most frequent question I get regarding this process is, *Who should I ask?* The answer is, it doesn't matter all that much. You don't have to know the person particularly well, or feel you have a lot in common. Anyone who can watch you in real time as you try out a different behavior will suffice, as long as you believe they will give you honest feedback.

The second most frequent question I get is, *What should I do if someone turns me down?* In my experience, this doesn't often happen unless your request has been unclear. But should it happen, you simply thank that person for considering it and then set about enlisting someone else. There's no need to interpret a refusal as rejection or a sign of disrespect. Maybe the person you asked is having a bad day, or mulling over a spat with her partner. Maybe they're simply not interested. Whatever the reason, you move on to someone else.

The more we practice this technique, the easier it becomes and the more areas we identify where we could use some help. Fairly soon, soliciting support will become our go-to response when we are trying to change things. This will increase the likelihood of our having sustainable success. We'll also have an easy tool for building new relationships and broadening our range of connections. And it's easier to feel encouraged when we know someone has our back.

SITUATIONAL PEER COACHING

Situational peer coaching operates similarly but the request is different. Instead of asking someone to watch you in a real-time situation, you say what you're trying to change and ask whether he or she has any tips.

Again, you don't have to know the person well, though in this case it's a good idea to ask someone who you believe is skillful at whatever you are trying to improve.

For example:

"Peter, do you have a moment?"

"Sure."

"I'm working hard to become more concise in how I communicate. I've had feedback that I sometimes meander. I've always admired how crisp and concise you are when you speak. I'm wondering whether you have any tips for me. Is there anything you do in preparation?"

The idea here is not to ask Peter to watch you. Rather, it's for you to get some ideas that could be helpful. Since you're asking him based on his observed expertise, it's doubtful that he will take offense at this reasonable and admiring request. More likely, he'll be flattered, and may take a new and more positive look at you. And you may get valuable insights and information.

When Peter gives you his thoughts, whether it's on the spot or a bit later, your job once again is just to listen. Certainly, you can dig down to learn more about any specific practices he shares. But this is no time to critique his offer, make promises of future action, or even hint at a *yes but*. Your only responsibility is to thank him and then think about what he said. You're free to act on his suggestion, either now or later. If you do, you may want to follow up and let him know how it worked out. This keeps you accountable without shifting undue responsibility onto him.

TRUTH IN ADVERTISING

Both these simple practices offer many advantages. You're more likely to do what you say because someone is watching. You have support as you try to move out of your comfort zone. You demonstrate your warmheartedness and show that you are open to change.

And you get to advertise the fact that you're changing.

This last is important. Often the people we work with (not to mention our families) tend to associate us with habits we've actually left behind. "Oh, she's always late to our meetings," a team member might say when in fact we've been making a huge effort and have not been late in six months. The problem is, people don't especially notice. They remember us as having been chronically late in the past, so continue to view us through this lens.

Articulating what we're trying to change and asking for help makes it easier for us to bring attention to our changed behavior because we let people know that we're working on it. Once they hear this, or hear it a few times, they'll start noticing and giving us credit. "Do you remember how Iris used to always be late? Boy, has she changed!"

Why did they suddenly notice? Because we cued them to notice by telling them what we're doing.

BEST PRACTICES

Whether you're soliciting real-time support or using situational peer coaching, here are a few things to keep in mind:

MAKE YOUR ASK SPECIFIC

If you're too general, you risk shifting the burden of figuring out what you mean to the other person. "I'm trying to be more concise when I present and I'm wondering whether you have a few tips" is an easier question to address than, "I need to be a more effective communicator. Can you help me?"

LIMIT YOUR TIME FRAME

People are busy, so when someone asks for help, they want a sense of how much time it will require. Specify that you're making a one-time request, and if appropriate, say when it would be helpful. "Can you watch me in our meeting next Monday morning?" is preferable to "Can you watch me in a meeting?" You don't want the person you're trying to enlist to wonder whether this will be an ongoing commitment.

SHOW GRATITUDE, BUT DON'T GO OVERBOARD

When you enlist someone's support, you are asking a favor, so you need to be appreciative even if what they offer isn't especially helpful. So a simple and heartfelt thank-you is sufficient. Resist the temptation to be effusive or festoon your thanks with unceasing comments about how amazingly wonderful the other person is. Balancing dignity with gratitude signals that you are worth their making an effort.

GETTING BETTER PLUS

Informal enlistment can be used to help us get better at anything, while also holding ourselves to account for becoming the people we want to be. But it's a particularly effective tool for building relationships across boundaries.

Active enlisters are able to forge unexpected connections, build robust and diverse webs of support, and instill the kind of trust that helps open up their entire culture. Active enlisters also become skilled at "going deep fast," spurring honest and consequential conversations with people they may hardly know that can have immediate or long-term value. Simply making a request demonstrates that we regard the person we are asking as a potential ally, someone we want to include in our circle of connection.

For all these reasons, informal enlistment is one of the most potent and accessible tools available for helping us rise together.

INFORMAL ENLISTMENT AS A TOOL
FOR ADDRESSING TRIGGERS

Situational peer coaching is especially effective at helping us confront triggers that might otherwise sow resentment and solidify division. Sean and Beth offer a great real-life example of how this can work.

"Beth, do you have a moment?"

"Sure. What's up?"

"I've been noticing that my attempts at humor in our meetings don't always land the way I intend. Sometimes I just fall flat, but other times people seem take offense, especially the women. I think our team works better when there's laughter in the room, which is why I crack a lot of jokes, but I don't want to come off as obnoxious. You seem able to get the whole team laughing in a way that feels very positive. Is there anything you do that might help me?"

This is a tough request to make, and Sean deserves credit for being honest and direct about a potentially fraught topic, especially as Beth may well confirm his intuition that he's not making the grade when it comes to humor, which is always going to feel like a big ouch. But by making himself vulnerable, he demonstrates both that he trusts her and that he's willing to change.

Beth then asks for clarification. "Sean, are you asking for examples of when your humor went wrong?"

"No, I'm not focused on the past. What's done is done. I need to look forward. What I'm asking is if there's anything *you* do, or don't do, that helps you use humor so skillfully."

Beth considers this for a moment, then says, "Thanks for the compliment; that makes me feel good. And your question helps me think about how I interact with the team. Two things come to mind. First, I rarely rely on jokes, partly because I'm bad at telling them and partly because a lot of jokes rely on making fun of someone, even if it's not explicit. Also, before I say anything I think might be funny, I always pause to ask myself *why* I want to say it. Is it to defuse tension? Is it to bring the group together? Or is it to make myself look clever? If that's the reason, and it often is, I let it go even if I think it's wildly amusing. Knowing what I hope to accomplish helps me exercise good judgment and keeps the team foremost in my mind."

"This is really helpful. Thank you!"

"If I think of anything else, I'll let you know. It means a lot to me that you'd ask about this."

Sean and Beth both benefit from this exchange. Sean comes away with two solid ideas that may help him become more skillful in using humor. Beth receives feedback about what makes her an effective team leader. This may help her act with more intention going forward.

Sean and Beth are also building trust with one another by directly addressing a potentially awkward situation. This strengthens them while also strengthening their team.

INFORMAL ENLISTMENT AS A TOOL FOR BUILDING INCLUSIVE HABITS

Soliciting real-time support is a particularly helpful means of practicing inclusive behaviors. Let's look at an example of how this can work.

Lars is a leader in his company's customer service unit. For the last two weeks, he's been working with his team to prepare a white paper on the pros and cons of continuing to offer a particular product. The senior management team is considering discontinuing it as part of a strategic alignment. But they want a sense of how customers might react.

Lulu, the squeaky wheel on the team, is a persistent advocate for keeping the product on the market, based on her frontline customer experience. So she's been active in documenting how the company can benefit from keeping it in circulation. But she's so gung ho that she's constantly pressing the team to add new arguments to the white paper, or expand upon points they've already made. Her incessant *what abouts* have slowed the process.

Lars has grown increasingly irritated with Lulu. She senses this and has responded by holding her ground. But now management has asked for the white paper and Lars needs to deliver it.

The issue is how to handle Lulu.

He's considering sending the paper on without any final tweaks. Or even circulating it for final comments without putting Lulu in the loop. Either of these approaches would get the job done, but would come with a cost. Lulu is one of Lars's biggest contributors and he sees little value in diminishing her engagement. Also, Lars originally promised that the project would be driven by consensus and doesn't want to go back on his word.

In this situation, Lars could benefit by informally enlisting Lulu to help him bring the project to conclusion.

Here's a possible script.

"Lulu, I've gotten word from upstairs that they need our white paper for their strategy meeting tomorrow morning. There's a little more work that could be done on it, so I'll be soliciting some comments, but we need to bring it to a close. You've been a great contributor, so I'm hoping you'll give me any thoughts you have on how to do this in a collaborative way. I can't promise I'll take all your suggestions, but I'd like to hear them. I need your help."

What's the upside to making this request? Lars will have persuasively expressed the extent to which he values Lulu's contributions and potentially defused some of the tension that's crept into their relationship. By enlisting her as an ally in both making the white paper better *and* in wrapping it up, he will have given her an added stake in the final product and so increased the likelihood that she'll advocate for it, with customers if need be. And he will have maintained his commitment to a collaborative style under challenging circumstances, which will help him grow as a leader.

A WORD ABOUT TRUST

We rise together by helping others rise, and they help us to rise in turn, so it's a good policy to practice informal enlistment as often as we can. We don't have to know the person we ask particularly well. In fact, informal enlistment is a powerful means for getting to know someone better.

And while trust is a positive, we don't need to trust the person we engage completely. After all, we're not making ourselves entirely vulnerable. We're simply being honest about what we're trying to achieve and inviting them to be part of it. Our risk is minimal, even though it might not feel that way if we're unaccustomed to making these kinds of requests.

Of course, it doesn't always work out as we hope or intend. Sometimes we don't receive support we ask for. Sometimes the person we ask has no interest in building the kind of virtuous circle of relationship and generosity that this process at its best can enable.

But that's fine. We can't control other peoples' responses. There's no need to judge someone who fails to reciprocate, criticize their response, or write them off. The point is that *we* tried. And simply practicing this skill helps us get better at it while also sending a message of trust and support.

CHAPTER TWELVE

Cultivating the Power of We

We rise together by understanding the true nature of power

Practicing inclusive behaviors and using informal enlistment expands our ability to build new relationships while fortifying and extending the relationships we have. We do so by employing honesty, demonstrating vulnerability without going overboard, and being direct. This augments our personal power regardless of our position, and bolsters anyone who is allied with us. In this way, we spread power even as we build it.

This is what we always want to bear in mind: as we become more powerful, those on our teams and in our circles of connection also benefit. Our customers and clients benefit, as do our organizations. There is great mutuality in power, except among those who either hoard it or use it to try to undermine and sideline others. But the careers (not to mention the lives) of such people are rarely satisfying or sustainable: they always have to watch their backs, and they constantly diminish the base of support from which they can draw.

Those for whom power is a zero-sum commodity often end up at zero, spiritually if not materially; isolated and bereft of support, or surrounded by strictly transactional allies or sycophants they cannot fully trust. And because they erode the power of those around them, they ultimately weaken the enterprise they presume to lead.

By contrast, those who recognize the give-and-take nature of power, and act in ways that support it, create cultures that strengthen rather than diminish over time. By making it possible to leverage the contributions, insights, knowledge, and connections of people at every level, they enable their organizations and all their associations to grow in value.

It is this reciprocal cultivation and dissemination of power—this dynamic sense of "we"—that enables us to rise together.

FOUR KINDS OF POWER

I learned what is still my best lesson about power from Ted Jenkins, an engineer who was one of the earliest hires at Intel, the storied semiconductor company that played a key role in the development of Silicon Valley. When I interviewed him for *The Web of Inclusion* back in 1994, Ted was described by people in the company as the keeper of the culture, the old hand who understood the internal dynamics that had made Intel a giant. His remarks not only shaped my thinking in *The Web*, they have continued to influence my understanding of nonpositional power ever since.

By nonpositional power, I mean power that is not strictly tied to position.

My question for Ted at the time was simple: what had made Intel so skilled at drawing innovative strategic ideas from people at every level and across units and divisions? The capacity to do this, especially during the Intel Inside realignment, when the company completely redefined both its market position and its customer base, erased to a surprising degree the standard industrial-era division between heads and hands: those whose job it is to originate ideas and those whose job it is to put ideas into practice.

This integration of thinking and doing, of strategy and execution, increased the company's capacity to leverage its considerable brainpower while engaging the insights of those in direct contact with customers and suppliers. Creating the conditions that supported this kind of broad engagement enabled the company to draw strategic ideas from across a wide spectrum.

Ted explained that Intel's strength traditionally lay in how it allowed resources to flow to wherever a problem or challenge needed to be met. In many companies, he said, "this just doesn't happen. I think that's because, in most organizations, resources tend to accumulate: they get stuck wherever someone holds a position of power. So what you end up with is a few powerful people who have more resources than they need or can use, while everybody else has to make do with less. It's static, irrational, and inefficient."

Ted noted that organizations have traditionally been structured to validate and exalt positional power. "The assumption is that the person at the top of the pyramid has, or should have, the power. But position is a crude way of allocating and measuring power because it ignores the diverse ways in which power actually operates in a complex organization."

We all understand this because we all recognize that every enterprise has what amounts to two org charts: the formal chart, which shows where everyone stands in the hierarchy or matrix, and the informal chart, which shows all the routes and tendrils that enable people to share information and get things done. Yet despite this recognition, companies often prefer to operate as if positional power were all that matters.

By contrast, said Ted, Intel had a history of explicitly acknowledging and supporting both formal and informal charts, which enabled alternative power bases to form and keep resources flowing. He then articulated the four kinds of power that he believed exist in and shape every organization, noting that each is an essential component of sustainable strength.

He cited:

- The power of position
- The power of expertise
- The power of connections
- The power of personal authority

Let's examine each of these in turn.

THE POWER OF POSITION

The power of position is determined by your title, your job description, your level, your place in the chain of command. It's where you stand on the official org chart. Your positional power gives you formal control over specific resources and the right to make specific decisions.

But while positional power has value and can be substantial, even overwhelming, it is nevertheless always extrinsic, unrelated to your individual talents or merit. However exalted or prestigious, your position is always simply the slot you are temporarily filling. It preexists your tenure and will endure after you have gone.

THE POWER OF EXPERTISE

The power of expertise is embedded in the skills and the knowledge you both bring to the job and develop over time, either through formal training or by daily practice. Because these skills are lodged in your brain and wired into your body, they are intrinsic to you in a way that positional power can never be. They are your personal source of embodied wisdom, the cumulative sum of your experience.

The great Japanese management thinker Ikujiro Nonaka notes that this kind of wisdom is innately self-renewing. He says, "Embodied knowledge is produced and consumed simultaneously. Its value *increases* with use rather than being depleted, as with industrial goods or commodities. Above all, it is a resource created by humans acting in relationship with one another and vested in their experience."

Even if your embedded skills and knowledge are not specified in your formal job description, they have the potential to benefit you and your organization. If you're a game developer with a personal passion for sports betting, you may have an opportunity to apply what you've learned from Caesars Sportsbook to the new product your team has in the works. If you're an event planner who formerly ran a catering business, you may have useful ideas about what kind of vendor can best support your upcoming event. If you're a leadership development manager with a background in improv, you may have special insights into experiential learning.

By offering what you know, you make clear your potential to contribute at a higher level in a way that serves you and everyone around you. However, if those with positional power hold the reins too tightly, the organization will struggle to leverage your expertise. When you volunteer your sportsbook knowledge, you may be told to stick to your subject. Or your caterer's insights may be rejected because dealing with those specific vendors is not your job.

This feels discouraging and disempowering, but because your expertise is intrinsic—that is, unique to you—your individual skills remain a source of potential power. As long as you do not lose confidence in what you have to contribute, and can clearly articulate the value you seek to provide, you can enhance the esteem in which you are held. And you can inspire others to expand their scope.

Or you can choose to take the talents you have refined on the company's time and dollar elsewhere. Though it's always a good idea to either evaluate or start building the support you'll need elsewhere before taking the leap, as we saw with Boris Groysberg's research in Chapter 7.

THE POWER OF CONNECTIONS

The power of connections is vested in your personal relationships. These include both the people you know and the one- to six-degrees-of-separation connections you can call upon when needed. A robust web of such connections operating throughout a company enables resources, ideas, and information to flow to where they can be most useful.

Having broad and diverse internal connections is also helpful for teams, making it easier for members to import needed skills and resources from unexpected places. For this reason, extending and strengthening your internal network will always empower you, your team, and your allies.

External connections can also be of great value. They help you build strong bonds in your community or your sector, elicit useful feedback from customers and clients, and develop information about emerging trends. Strong social or traditional media connections, used judiciously, can amplify the impact of what you are contributing, providing serious support for your allies and your organization.

For all these reasons, your connections are a key component of your value. Again, this remains true even if your organization fails to leverage them because, like the power of expertise, the power of connections is always intrinsic to you.

THE POWER OF PERSONAL AUTHORITY

The power of personal authority resides in your ability to inspire trust and respect among those you work with, regardless of the position you hold. Personal authority may be and often is wildly disproportionate to positional power: the supply chain clerk who helps identify a new distribution link, the admin who serves as a top executive's eyes and ears. Having strong personal authority often spurs senior colleagues to seek out your observations and judgment, which increases their power as well as yours.

Since people tend to share information with those they trust, having strong personal authority can result in your being a gold mine of information. Having access to information augments your power, though if you try to display this power by sharing what you know indiscriminately, you risk losing it. Indiscretion and gossip can destroy personal authority overnight, so you want to treat it as a precious resource. Personal authority is always intrinsic, but only if you remain a trusted and reliable ally for those around you.

Ted Jenkins also noted that, in toxic organizations, leaders tend to view the broad distribution of expertise, connections, and personal authority as a threat to their own positional power rather than a resource they can draw on to make the enterprise stronger. Their reluctance to nurture other kinds of power results in widespread demotivation and a diminished capacity for innovation and growth. Although these weaknesses may take time to manifest, information and resource logjams are the most typical immediate consequences for organizations that overprivilege positional power.

Ted believed that Intel was skilled at nurturing nonpositional power in part because its matrixed structure enabled people to move around a lot. This gave everyone the opportunity to build diverse connections and varied kinds of expertise. He also viewed Intel's low turnover as a key factor. "Positional power tends to predominate when people don't stay with the organization for very long. You lose capacity if people keep coming and going."

INFLUENCE POTENTIAL

Peter Drucker had a useful definition of power. He described it as "influence potential." He believed that we are powerful only insofar as we are able to influence people and events to create the outcomes we deem desirable. Looked at through this lens, we see that power is not force, though those in high positions at times confuse the two.

Of course, if we control the resources used to reward or penalize others, we can usually get others to go along. But they may do so grudgingly, limiting their participation to what they believe is absolutely required. Some part of them will always resist.

This truth reflects the principle of polarity we observe in nature. The strong exertion of any force always spurs a counterreaction, as the system seeks to rebalance itself. Since humans are part of the natural world, this principle also operates in society: in families, organizations, communities, and among nations, as history teaches. By stirring resistance, those who attempt to enforce by power rather than engage it by using the subtler skills of influence bring chaos to the world.

Drucker's definition aligns with the four kinds of power described by Ted Jenkins. We may or may not have the positional power to make a specific decision. Yet through the skillful employment of our connections, expertise, and personal authority, we can nevertheless influence the direction of the enterprise of which we are a part.

By intentionally developing and honing our influence potential, we also participate in shaping the culture. And every one of us can play a role. Culture is not HR's job, or the leader's job. It's *our* job, regardless of the positional power we hold.

This is particularly true if our aim is to create a culture of belonging, in which people at every level can flourish. That's because a culture of belonging can never be mandated from the top. Instead, the actions, relationships, and capacity to create trust of individuals at every level are required to build it.

Let's revisit our definition from the Introduction.

A culture of belonging is one in which the largest possible percentage of people:

- Feel ownership in the organization, viewing it as "we" not "they"
- Believe they are valued for their *potential* as well as their contributions
- Perceive that how they matter is not strictly tied to their positional power

THE PRACTICE OF INFLUENCE

The inclusive behaviors described in Chapter 10 give us a way to build and exercise our nonpositional power. So does the practice of informal enlistment described in Chapter 11.

- By using the language of *we*, we help others see beyond the "they."
- By asking others what they believe they are really good at or what skills they don't get a chance to use, we let them know that we value their potential.
- By helping others build and expand their connections, expertise, and personal authority, we show that we recognize the full scope of who they are, rather than identifying them solely with their positional power.

And so we recommend others. We honor the squeaky wheel. We practice active listening. We invest in one another's success.

And we let others know exactly what we're trying to do, even as we do it: *I'm trying to become a better listener. How do you think I'm doing? Do you have any ideas for me?*

Taking these sorts of actions across barriers of gender, race, sexuality, level, and division enables us to erode those barriers and build the broadest possible range of alliances. By expanding our webs to be more inclusive, more diverse, more knowledge-rich, and more robust, we create new sources of power that distribute influence, disseminate power, and augment our own energy.

And by demonstrating generosity through simple actions, we align ourselves with the dynamic power of grace. Grace operates beyond considerations of merit to bestow blessings that are not earned but may be shared and multiplied, as John Baldoni writes.

Understanding the true nature of power can help us feel more comfortable using it because we recognize it as a potential force for good. In my experience, women, even those who hold substantial positions, often regard power as a negative. They do so in the same way and for the same reasons that Anna Fels's patients regarded ambition as a negative: they've seen it exercised badly. "I'm not interested in power," women tell me, "I just want to have a satisfying career." As if power and satisfaction were mutually exclusive.

Although less frequently, I also hear men disclaim any interest in power: "I just want to be left alone to do my job." As if just serving as a cog in a wheel could be all that rewarding, or support a life of meaning and purpose.

The ability to influence events in a positive way is one of the most satisfying experiences available to humans. Feeling powerless is not.

Marshall Goldsmith has a great question for people who insist they have no interest in power, are unwilling to pursue it or proudly disdainful of those who do.

He asks, "Do you believe the world would be a better place if you and people like you had more power?"

Most people will say that they do.

"Then why would you not try to become more powerful? Don't you want the world to be a better place?"

And so I close with the question:

Don't you?

Notes

Most of the stories and practices I share in this book derive from my own experience and so do not require citations. Books, articles, and quoted interviews with experts do.

Introduction

Page xiv: Gallup survey, see https://fundacionprolongar.org/wp-content/uploads/2019/07/State-of-the-Global-Workplace_Gallup-Report.pdf.

Pages xv–xvii: For more on increased confidence and solidarity among women in the workplace, see my article "The Evolution of Women's Leadership," *Strategy+Business*, July 28, 2020, https://www.strategy-business.com/article/The-evolution-of-womens-leadership.

Chapter One

Page 5: See Marshall Goldsmith, *Triggers: Creating Behavior That Lasts—Becoming the Person You Want to Be* (New York: Crown Business, 2015).

Page 12: My conversation with Chris Cappy.

Page 14: Author interview with Marshall Goldsmith.

Chapter Two

Pages 23ff: For more on aikido as a strategic tool, see my article on Richard Strozzi-Heckler, "The Dance of Power," *Strategy+Business*, November 28, 2007, https://www.strategy-business.com/article/07406.

Also see two of Strozzi's wonderful books:

Holding the Center: Sanctuary in a Time of Confusion (Berkeley: North Atlantic Books, 1997).

In Search of the Warrior Spirit: Teaching Awareness Disciplines to the Green Berets, 4th ed. (Berkeley: Blue Snake Books, 2007).

Pages 27ff: My conversation with Colonel Diane Ryan.

Page 30: Sun Tzu is essential reading for anyone who wants to approach his or her career in an intentional and strategic way. Among the many translations, I prefer *The Art of War: The Denma Translation* (Boston: Shambhala Classics, 2001). For more on "taking whole," see pages 65–81 and other citations.

Two other books I view as key for strategic career development:

The Tao of Power: Lao Tzu's Classic Guide to Leadership, Influence and Excellence, trans. R. L. Wing (New York: Doubleday, 1986) (this translation is the one).

Niccolò Machiavelli, *The Prince*, trans. Tim Parks (New York: Penguin Classics, 2009) (again, this translation makes sense of a thorny classic).

Pages 31–32: On men being more willing to speak up in meetings, see multiple studies summarized in Lydia Smith, "How Men Dominate in Meetings," Yahoo News, April 10, 2019, https://news.yahoo.com /stark-reality-men-dominate-talking-meetings-113112910.html.

For how this extends into the virtual workplace, see, for example, Alisha Haridasani Gupta, "It's Not Just You: In Online Meetings Women Can't Get a Word In," *New York Times*, April 14, 2020, https://www.nytimes .com/2020/04/14/us/zoom-meetings-gender.html.

Chapter Three

Pages 40ff: Anna Fels, *Necessary Dreams: Ambition in Women's Changing Lives* (New York: Anchor Books, 2004).

Pages 42ff: On the continuing negative perceptions of women who are assertive or ambitious, see Christine L. Exley and Judd B. Kessler, "The Gender Gap in Self-Promotion," National Bureau of Economic Research, 2021, https://www.nber.org/papers/w26345.

On the role of performance reviews in supporting these perceptions, see Kristen Bahler, "Are Performance Reviews Sexist? New Research Says Yes," *Money Magazine*, January, 23, 2020, https://money.com /performance-reviews-are-sexist/.

Interesting article from *Forbes* in the wake of the 2016 US election in which Hilary Clinton was routinely described as "pathologically ambitious": Liz Elting, "The High Cost of Ambition: Why Women Are Being Held Back for Thinking Big," April 24, 2017, https://www.forbes.com /sites/lizelting/2017/04/24/the-high-cost-of-ambition-why-women-are -held-back-for-thinking-big/?sh=2a4d18a31ee6.

On women and emotion, see multiple examples, Quentin Fottrel, "'Women Are Judged for Being Emotional'—Yet It's More Acceptable for Men to Get Upset and Angry, Female Executives Say," Marketwatch,

November 29, 2019, https://www.marketwatch.com/story/serena
-williams-got-angry-at-the-us-open-final-and-paid-a-heavy-price
working-women-say-this-sounds-eerily-familiar-2018-09-10.

Pages 45ff: my conversation with Terry Jackson.

Pages 50ff: my conversation with Jeffrey Hull.

Pages 51ff: Stephen Covey, *The Seven Habits of Highly Effective People: Powerful Lessons in Personal Change*, 30th anniversary ed. (New York: Simon & Schuster, 2020).

Chapter Four

Pages 53ff: This story about Alan Mulally has appeared in various forms in various books. However, I took it from watching him deliver a four-hour workshop at the Scottsdale Marriott in March 2018.

Pages 57–60 and 70–71: Sandy Stosz's story from her book *Breaking Ice and Breaking Glass: Leading in Uncharted Waters* (Virginia Beach, VA: Koëhler Books, 2021). Also from my exchanges with her.

Pages 61ff: Katty Kay and Claire Shipman, *The Confidence Code: The Science and Art of Self-Assurance—What Women Should Know* (New York: Harper Business, 2014).

Pages 62ff: Tomas Chamorro-Premuzic, *Why Do So Many Incompetent Men Become Leaders? (And How to Fix It)* (Boston: Harvard Business Review, 2019).

Chapter Five

Page 74: Molly Tschang's excellent podcast *Say It Skillfully* is a great resource for anyone seeking to improve their communications fluency, https://www.sayitskillfully.com.

Pages 76–79: I developed the distinction between notice, value, and connecting the dots while researching *The Female Vision: Women's Real Power at Work*, Sally Helgesen and Julie Johnson (San Francisco, CA: Berrett-Kohler, 2010).

In the book, Julie and I sought to identify what was singular about women's vision in an effort to more clearly define their strategic value. We found that women's capacity for what we called "broad spectrum notice" was a foundational element of how they see things. This observation is fully developed on pages 41–56 of that book.

Pages 77–79: For more on Brooksley Born, see pages 32–34 of *The Female Vision*. Born's principled stand was mostly overlooked at the time, but it is widely referenced in response to the 2008 financial crisis.

Pages 79–80: On women being perceived as diffuse, most studies show women use more words than men. See, for example, Catherine Aponte, "Do

Women Really Talk More Than Men?" *Psychology Today* (blog), October 10, 2019, https://www.psychologytoday.com/us/blog/marriage-equals/201910/do-women-really-talk-more-men.

Other studies show that men use more words. In my experience, there's a simple explanation. I find men more likely to speak in a wide range of situations, typically because they have higher status with the group. Although women often hold back, they are more likely to go into detail when they do speak up.

Page 80: My conversation with Tom Peters. See also his wonderful *Excellence Now: Extreme Humanism* (Chicago: Networlding, 2021).

Pages 81ff: My my conversation with Lindsey Pollak.

Pages 84ff: My conversation with Bev Wright.

Pages 86ff: Jay Caspian Kang is brilliant on the awkwardness of categories in his excellent weekly newsletter in the *New York Times*, https://www.nytimes.com/by/jay-caspian-kang.

See also Caspian Kang on how this awkwardness impacts how we talk about sports, particularly basketball: "Ball Don't Lie," *New York Review of Books*, September 24, 2020, https://www.nybooks.com/articles/2020/09/24/nba-basketball-dont-lie/.

I am also guided in my thinking about racial and ethnic categorization by Isabel Wilkerson, *Caste: The Origins of Our Discontents* (New York: Random House, 2020).

Pages 86ff: Bill Wiersma, *The Power of Professionalism: The Seven Mind-Sets That Drive Performance and Build Trust* (Dover, NH: Ravel Media, 2011).

Chapter Six

Page 93: Marshall Goldsmith, *Triggers: Creating Behavior That Lasts—Becoming the Person You Want to Be* (New York: Crown Business, 2015.

Pages 94ff: I am grateful to my colleague Patricia Gorton for sharing the story of Erica and Louis.

Page 98: "Decisions are made," from my conversations with Peter Drucker in the years before his death.

Page 102: My conversation with Marshall Goldsmith.

Page 103: Websites for Talent Management and HR provide excellent documentation of these patterns of unfairness; see, for example, https://www.tlnt.com/the-hidden-bias-in-performance-reviews/.

Pages 106ff: For more detail and analysis, see Sally Helgesen, *The Web of Inclusion* (New York: Doubleday Currency, 1995).

Page 109: My conversation with Tom Kolditz.

Chapter Seven

Pages 112ff: On the first widespread use of a grapevine as a mode of communication in the Civil War, see, for example, https://www.etymonline.com/word/grapevine.

For origins among enslaved and Native American networks, see https://www.phrases.org.uk/meanings/heard-it-through-the-grapevine.html.

Pages 113–115: My conversation with Bill Carrier.

Page 116: On Xerox as the first ERG, see, for example, Boston College Center for Work and Family, Executive Briefing Series, https://www.bc.edu/content/dam/files/centers/cwf/research/publications3/executive briefingseries-2/ExecutiveBriefing_EmployeeResourceGroups.pdf.

Pages 117ff: On the Olori Sisterhood, see Jeffery C. Mays, November 27, 2020, *New York Times*, https://www.nytimes.com/2020/11/27/nyregion/black-women-politics-olori-sisterhood.html.

Pages 119ff: My conversation with Eddie Turner.

Pages 122ff: See Boris Groysberg, *Chasing Stars: The Myth of Talent and the Portability of Performance* (Princeton, NJ: Princeton University Press, 2010). In my view, one of the best books ever written on talent and culture. See especially his research on female analysts, Chapter 8.

Pages 124ff: On referent groups, see Marshall Goldsmith and R. Roosevelt Thomas Jr., Chapter 6 in *Human Resources in the 21st Century*, ed. Marc Effron, Robert Gandossy, and Marshall Goldsmith (Hoboken, NJ: John Wiley & Sons, 2003), 51.

Chapter Eight

Pages 134ff: My conversation with Tom Peters.

Page 137: For Madeleine Albright, see, for example, Mike Snider, "Madeleine Albright: Diplomat Used Brooches, Costume Jewelry Pins to 'Deliver a Message,'" *USA Today*, March 23, 2022, https://www.usatoday.com/story/news/politics/2022/03/23/madeleine-albright-secretary-state-used-brooches-pin-diplomacy/7144400001/.

Page 139: On humor initiation and appreciation, see, for example, Christie Nicolson, "The Humor Gap," *Scientific American*, October 10, 2012, https://www.scientificamerican.com/article/the-humor-gap-2012-10-23/.

Pages 140ff: See Jennifer Aaker and Naomi Bagdonas, *Humor, Seriously: Why Humor is a Secret Weapon in Business and Life (And Anyone Can Harness It. Even You.)* (New York: Doubleday Currency, 2020).

The authors also have an excellent TED Talk and did a LinkedIn Live with Marshall Goldsmith, https://www.youtube.com/watch?v=Aq21F2DrU9M&t=6s.

Page 143: My conversation with Molly Tschang.

Chapter Nine

Pages 145ff: For Milbank's excellent column, see Dana Milbank, "A #MeToo for Clueless Men," *Washington Post*, October 27, 2017, https://www.washingtonpost.com/opinions/a-metoo-for-clueless-men/2017/10/27/8cc06b00-bb52-11e7-a908-a3470754bbb9_story.html.

Page 150: For Zucker story, there are many reports. See, for example, Emily Steel et al., "Jeff Zucker's Downfall at CNN: Ethical Lapses and Falling Ratings," *New York Times*, February 15, 2022, https://www.nytimes.com/2022/02/15/business/jeff-zucker-cnn.html.

Pages 150–151: On employees failing to report relationships or harassment, see Namely, "The Importance of Anonymous Reporting in the Workplace," August 18, 2021, https://blog.namely.com/anonymous-reporting-workplace.

Pages 152ff: See Elizabeth Spiers, "My Workplace Romance Was a Brilliant Mistake," *New York Times*, February 12, 2022, https://www.nytimes.com/2022/02/12/opinion/culture/jeff-zucker-workplace-romance.html.

Pages 154–155: See Didion's essay "On Self-Respect" in *Slouching Toward Bethlehem* (New York: FSG Classics, 2008); original essay from 1968.

Pages 156–157: On office romance, see Amy Gallo, "How to Approach an Office Romance and How Not To," *Harvard Business Review*, February 14, 2019, https://hbr.org/2019/02/how-to-approach-an-office-romance-and-how-not-to.

Chapter Ten

Pages 163–165: Pamela Newkirk, *Diversity, Inc: The Failed Promise of a Billion-Dollar Business* (New York: Bold Type Books, 2019). This well-researched and well-argued book needs to be more influential.

Page 168: On Peter Drucker being the last to speak. I saw this demonstrated on many occasions. See also Drucker's *The Effective Executive: The Definitive Guide to Getting the Right Things Done* (New York: Harper Business Essentials, 2006).

Page 169: On the influence of Japanese integrated manufacturing model, see, for example, Maryann Keller, *Rude Awakening: The Rise Fall and Struggle for Recovery of General Motors* (New York: William Morrow, 1989).

Page 171: For research on C-suite failing to lead those at less-senior levels on inclusion, see "If CEOs Want to Promote Diversity, They Have to

'Walk the Talk,'" The Conversation, November 30, 2021, https://the conversation.com/if-ceos-want-to-promote-diversity-they-have-to -walk-the-talk-172275.

Pages 172ff: For my case study of Frances Hesselbein's leadership style, see Sally Helgesen, *The Female Advantage, Women's Ways of Leadership* (New York: Doubleday Currency, 1990); also Frances Hesselbein's "Merit Badge in Leadership," *Strategy+Business*, September 2015, https://www .strategy-business.com/article/00332.

Page 176: John Baldoni, *Grace: A Leader's Guide to a Better Us* (Pensacola, FL: Indigo River, 2019).

Pages 176–177: Chester Elton and Adrian Gostick's many books are inspiring and full of practical advice. See, for example, *Leading with Gratitude: Eight Leadership Practices for Extraordinary Results* (New York: Harper Collins, 2020).

Pages 179–180: My conversation with Ruth Gotian.

Pages 182–183: My conversation with Tom Peters.

Pages 183ff: My conversation with Mike Kaufmann.

Chapter Eleven

Pages 207–210: As noted, Marshall Goldsmith has taught some version of Feed-forward in many of the leadership programs he has delivered over the last twenty years. I built upon his work to develop the practice of informal enlistment, which I've refined in hundreds of workshops and seminars.

Pages 210ff: Peer coaching and especially situational peer coaching are practices I use in many settings as both facilitator and coach.

Chapter Twelve

Pages 200ff: Ted Jenkins's insights on nonpositional power are set forth and explored in the "Intel Inside" chapter of my book *The Web of Inclusion* (New York: Doubleday Currency, 1995).

Page 203: For more on Nonaka, see my profile of him, "The Practical Wisdom of Ikujiro Nonaka," *Strategy+Business*, November 25, 2008, https://sally helgesen.com/2008/11/the-practical-wisdom-of-ikujiro-nonaka-2/.

Page 206: I could not find a citation for Drucker on influence potential, but Marshall Goldsmith, who spent much time with Drucker and worked with him, credits him with saying this on many occasions.

Page 206: On the principle of polarity and how it influences power, see *The Tao of Power: Lao Tzu's Classic Guide to Leadership, Influence and Excellence*, trans. R. L. Wing (New York: Doubleday, 1986).

Page 208: John Baldoni, *Grace: A Leader's Guide to a Better Us* (Pensacola, FL: Indigo River, 2019).